Mama's FAMILY cookbook

Mama's FAMILY cookbook

Family recipes from
the Italian kitchen

First published in 2013
LOVE FOOD is an imprint of Parragon Books Ltd

Parragon
Chartist House,
15-17 Trim Street,
Bath, BA1 1HA, UK

www.parragon.com/lovefood

ISBN: 978-1-78186-810-2
Printed in China

Design concept by Sabine Vonderstein, Cologne, Germany, with additional design work by Sian Williams
New photography and home economy: Mike Cooper and Lincoln Jefferson
New recipes: Beverly Le Blanc
Mama text: Dominic Utton
Senior Commissioning Editor: Cheryl Warner

Mama and all characters mentioned in this book are entirely fictitious. Any similarity to any person, living or dead, is purely coincidental and unintended.

Notes for the Reader
This book uses both metric and imperial measurements. Follow the same units of measurement throughout; do not mix metric and imperial. All spoon measurements are level: teaspoons are assumed to be 5 ml, and tablespoons are assumed to be 15 ml. Unless otherwise stated, milk is assumed to be full fat, eggs and individual vegetables are medium, and pepper is freshly ground black pepper. Unless otherwise stated, all root vegetables should be washed in plain water and peeled prior to using. For best results, use a food thermometer when cooking meat and poultry – check the latest government guidelines for current advice.

Garnishes, decorations and serving suggestions are all optional and not necessarily included in the recipe ingredients or method. The times given are an approximate guide only. Recipes using raw or very lightly cooked eggs should be avoided by infants, the elderly, pregnant women, convalescents and anyone suffering from an illness. Pregnant and breastfeeding women are advised to avoid eating peanuts and peanut products. Sufferers from nut allergies should be aware that some of the ready-made ingredients used in the recipes in this book may contain nuts. Always check the packaging before use.

Picture Acknowledgements
The publisher would like to thank the following for permission to reproduce copyright material on the following pages: Cover (Mama image): Mrs. Luisa Pierotti © CARLO BAVAGNOLI/Getty Images; page 8: Tomatoes, glass, teapot on table © Anna Nemoy (Xaomena)/Getty Images; page 9 (heart image): Rose petals forming heart shape symbol © 2009 Chaulafanita/Getty Images. All other incidentals are Istockphoto images.

Contents

Introduction

Ciao amici! Welcome to Mama's Italian Family Cookbook — not just a collection of recipes from my own kitchen, but a scrapbook of family wisdom and a little insight into my life.

This is the second cookbook I've written and this one is all about recreating the energy, ambience, love and, of course, wonderful food that is only found in the heart of a true Italian family. Inside you will find many *molto delizioso* recipes, of course — but also so much more. My cookbooks are not just about preparing meals: they're a whole way of life, a *filosofia* for *la bella vita*.

For me, there is no distinction between the cooking and the cook — the feelings, the passion, the love and the experiences of the person making the recipes all go into the food... and so the cook becomes a part of the recipe! All of which means — to understand my food is to understand me. And if there is one word that would sum me up, it's *famiglia*. Family is everything to me. That's why they call me Mama!

But I'm talking too quickly. First things first! Let me tell you about myself. I'm the head of a large, noisy, happy household here in a small village in Apulia, a province in the south of Italy. I've been married to Alberto for nearly 60 years — as long as your Queen has been sitting on the throne!

We live a simple life in Apulia — we don't ask for much, and we make our own happiness. And nowhere is that more true than with our *famiglia*.

Together Alberto and I have six *bambini*, 22 *nipoti*, or grandchildren, and 12 *pronipoti*, or great grandchildren. Every year brings another baby! And if that is a blessing, it is also a miracle that each of our great grandchildren are beautiful boys. Alberto often jokes that together one day our *pronipoti* will form a football team to rival the divine AC Milan side of 1989! I say they will be better.

Of course, I may be the head of a family of over 40 strong (and I don't include myself or Alberto in that, nor our many cousins, nephews, nieces... all of whom can often be found sitting at our table or harassing Mama in the kitchen!) but naturally I'm not cooking for all of them every day. Our *bambini* have families of their own now.

But still — Mama never cooks a lonely meal. Our eldest boys, Marco and Filippo, still work the same olive groves that Alberto used to tend.

And our youngest two, Maria and Lucia, married men from the same village and live within earshot on a clear day. It is a rare day that will not see six or seven hungry mouths for me to feed!

PONTE VECCHIO

LATTE

8

I've lived in this village all of my life — and my Mama, her Mama and her Mama before her all did the same. Tradition is *molto importante* here.

And nowhere is this more clearly seen than in the kitchen. Learning how to feed a family is a skill and a passion that is passed down the generations. It is a source of pride with me that I have always put beautiful, healthy food on my table — and my family have grown strong and beautiful themselves as a result.

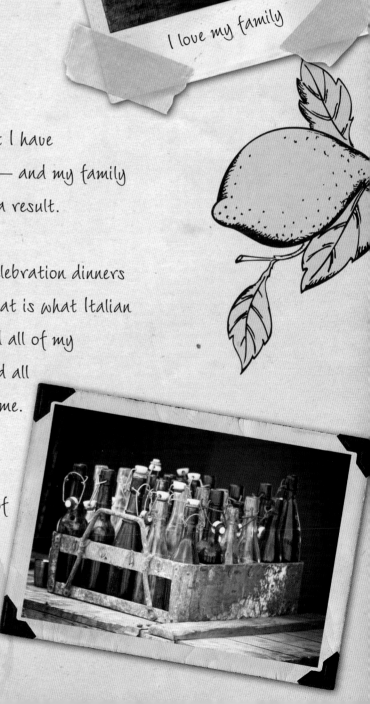

I love my family

From simple suppers when times are hard to celebration dinners fit for kings and queens — coming together to eat is what Italian family life is all about. All of my experience and all of my passion is captured in the following pages — and all the experience and passion of those who taught me. And believe me when I tell you I had the best teachers in all of Italy — my Mama, and her Mama before her. It is not simply a collection of recipes, it's an expression of Italian family life.

Buon appetito!

Eccellente Antipasti & Starters

Antipasti means 'before the meal' in Italian and is the traditional first course of any family dinner. This starter is the beginning of the meal, when anticipation is at its highest and, for the chef, it is the first chance you have to show what you're made of. From delicious calamari, spicy olives or garlic bread to broths and soups, it is a time not for satisfying appetites — but rather for whetting them still further for the delights yet to come! Creating *eccellente* antipasti sets the tone for the whole meal. It should be like the first kiss of a passionate love affair: beautiful in itself, but only a mere taster for the joys to follow. And remember the wise words of my Mama: 'la più grande opera inizia con la semplice nota' — even the grandest operas begin with the simplest notes.

Scarpariello
- - - - - - - - - -
Chicken Wings

1. Mix together the flour and paprika in a wide dish. Season the chicken wings with salt and pepper, then dredge them in the flour mixture, shaking off the excess.

2. Heat the oil in a large, deep frying pan over a medium—high heat. Add as many chicken wings as will fit in the pan in a single layer, and fry for 3—5 minutes, until golden brown on both sides. Remove from the pan and set aside. Add extra oil to the pan, if needed, and repeat until all the wings are fried.

3. Pour off all but 1 tablespoon of the oil. Add the sausages to the pan and fry for 3—5 minutes, until brown all over. Remove from the pan and set aside.

4. Pour off all but 1 tablespoon of the oil from the pan. Add the onion and red peppers and stir for 3—5 minutes, until soft. Add the cherry peppers and garlic and stir for a further 2 minutes, until the garlic is soft.

5. Return the chicken and sausages to the pan. Stir in the stock, wine, lemon juice and chilli flakes (if using), and season with salt and pepper. Bring to the boil, cover the pan, reduce the heat to low and simmer for 15—20 minutes, until the wings are cooked through and the juices run clear when you cut into one.

6. Using a slotted spoon, transfer the wings, sausages, red peppers and cherry peppers to warmed plates. Bring the liquid in the pan to the boil, then spoon over the meat. Garnish with parsley and serve immediately.

SERVES 4

2 tbsp plain flour
¼ tsp hot paprika
24 chicken wings, trimmed
2 tbsp olive oil, plus extra
   if needed
4 spicy Italian sausages,
   cut into 4-cm/1½-inch pieces
1 onion, thinly sliced
2 red peppers, deseeded and
   sliced
4 pickled cherry peppers,
   sliced
4 garlic cloves, sliced
125 ml/4 fl oz chicken stock
125 ml/4 fl oz dry white wine
2 tbsp lemon juice
pinch of dried chilli flakes
   (optional)
salt and pepper
4 tbsp chopped fresh flat-leaf
   parsley, to garnish

Calamari Fritti
Fried Calamari

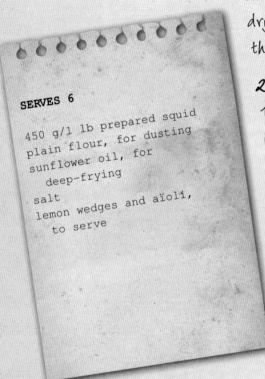

SERVES 6

450 g/1 lb prepared squid
plain flour, for dusting
sunflower oil, for
   deep-frying
salt
lemon wedges and aïoli,
   to serve

1. Slice the squid into 1-cm/½-inch rings and halve the tentacles if large. Rinse under cold running water and pat dry with kitchen paper. Dust the squid rings with flour so that they are lightly coated.

2. Heat the oil in a deep-fat fryer or heavy-based saucepan to 180–190°C/350–375°F, or until a cube of bread browns in 30 seconds. Fry the squid rings, in batches, turning several times, for 2–3 minutes, or until golden brown and crisp all over. Do not overcook as the squid will become tough and rubbery rather than moist and tender.

3. Remove with a slotted spoon and drain well on kitchen paper. Keep warm while you fry the remaining squid rings.

4. Sprinkle the fried squid rings with salt and serve piping hot, accompanied by lemon wedges for squeezing over and aïoli for dipping.

Mamá's Tip:
If you like your calamari to have a bit more zing, add a pinch of cayenne pepper to the flour.

Arancini

- - - - - - - - - - - - - -

Risotto Balls

1. Heat the oil with 25 g/1 oz of the butter in a deep saucepan. Add the onion and cook, stirring frequently, for 5 minutes, or until softened.

2. Add the rice and mix to coat in oil and butter. Cook, stirring constantly, for 2—3 minutes, or until the grains are translucent.

3. Gradually add the hot stock, a ladleful at a time. Add more liquid as the rice absorbs each addition. Cook, stirring, for 20 minutes, or until all the liquid is absorbed and the rice is creamy.

4. Remove from the heat and add the remaining butter. Mix well, then stir in the Parmesan until it melts. Season to taste with salt and pepper. Leave to cool completely.

5. Place 1 tablespoon of the risotto in the palm of your hand. Top with a cube of mozzarella, then place another tablespoon of risotto on top. Press together to form a ball, making sure that the filling is fully enclosed. Repeat until all the risotto and mozzarella have been used up.

6. Chill the risotto balls for 10 minutes, then dip in the egg. Drain and coat in the breadcrumbs, shaking off any excess. Chill for 10 minutes.

7. Heat enough oil for deep-frying in a large saucepan or deep-fat fryer to 180—190°C/350—375°F, or until a cube of bread browns in 30 seconds. Carefully drop in the risotto balls, in batches, and cook for 5 minutes, until golden brown.

8. Remove the risotto balls from the oil with a slotted spoon, then drain on kitchen paper. Leave to cool slightly before serving.

SERVES 4

1 tbsp olive oil
40 g/1½ oz butter
1 small onion, finely chopped
450 g/1 lb risotto rice
2 litres/3½ pints vegetable
  stock
55 g/2 oz freshly grated
  Parmesan cheese
115 g/4 oz mozzarella cheese,
  cubed
1 egg, beaten
115 g/4 oz fresh breadcrumbs
oil, for deep-frying
salt and pepper

Mama's guide to the perfect family party

They say the perfect party needs three things: the best people, the best food and the best hostess. Well, when the guests are famiglia and the hostess is Mama, you're more than halfway there! And, of course, with Mama's recipes, the food is certain to be the best too...

So how does Mama host the perfect family party? Follow my easy pointers and you can't go too far wrong.

First, remember — parties are supposed to be fun! Even if organizing a big get-together can feel a little stressante, always keep in mind why you're doing it. These are your nearest and dearest, your most beloved. Everything will be fine.

Families, of course, expand — and although in Apulia everyone knows each other's business, there may still be girlfriends, boyfriends, partners or friends who don't know everyone present. Mama has a trick when introducing two strangers — say their names and then think of something they have in common: 'Beppe, this is Alfredo. Alfredo's cousin works with you in Napoli, I believe...'

It's not just about you. Sure, you're the hostess — but everyone's here to have a good time. Let the party flow to its own rhythm: you don't have to be everywhere at once!

Hostessing a party does not mean spending all your time in the kitchen. You should enjoy yourself too! Relax and have a glass of Chianti, once all the main jobs are done.

Evviva!

Although things should develop at their own pace, be strict with the food. If it is a stand-up party, keep the nibbles well stocked and be sure all your guests sample some. If you are sitting to eat, call everyone to the table promptly.

Finally and più importante: don't forget to keep the vino flowing for everyone else! This is Alberto's department — but Mama likes to make sure he's keeping everyone's glass topped up!

Bruschetta con Funghi
Mushroom Bruschetta

SERVES 4

4 slices sourdough bread,
  such as Pugliese
3 garlic cloves, 1 halved and
  2 finely chopped
3 tbsp extra virgin olive oil
225 g/8 oz mixed wild mushrooms,
  such as porcini, chanterelles
  and field mushrooms
25 g/1 oz butter
1 small onion, finely chopped
50 ml/2 fl oz dry white wine
salt and pepper
2 tbsp chopped fresh flat-leaf
  parsley, to garnish

1. Preheat the grill to medium. Toast the bread slices under the preheated grill on both sides.

2. Rub the bread with the garlic halves and drizzle with 2 tablespoons of the oil. Keep warm.

3. Wipe the mushrooms thoroughly to remove any trace of soil and slice any large ones.

4. Heat the remaining oil with half of the butter in a frying pan. Add the mushrooms and cook over a medium heat, stirring, for 3—4 minutes, until soft. Remove with a slotted spoon and keep warm.

5. Heat the remaining butter in the frying pan. Add the onion and chopped garlic and cook, stirring, for 3—4 minutes, until soft. Add the wine, stir and leave to bubble for 2—3 minutes, until reduced.

6. Return the mushrooms to the frying pan and heat through. The sauce should be thick enough to glaze the mushrooms. Season to taste with salt and pepper.

7. Pile the mushrooms on top of the toasted bread, scatter over the parsley and serve immediately.

Pane all' Aglio
Garlic Bread

1. Preheat the oven to 180°C/350°F/Gas Mark 4.

2. Mix together the butter, garlic and parsley in a bowl until well combined. Season with pepper to taste and mix well.

3. Make several lengthways cuts in the bread but be careful not to cut all the way through.

4. Spread the flavoured butter over one side of each cut and place the loaf on a large sheet of aluminium foil on a baking sheet.

5. Wrap up the bread in the aluminium foil and bake in the preheated oven for 10—15 minutes, or until the butter melts and the bread is piping hot. Leave to cool on a wire rack for 5 minutes, then serve immediately.

Mama's Tip:
Replace half of the parsley with chopped fresh basil, if the bread will be eaten with a tomato-based dish.

SERVES 6

150 g/5½ oz butter, softened
3 garlic cloves, crushed
2 tbsp chopped fresh flat-
leaf parsley
pepper
1 large or 2 small sticks
of Italian bread

Bruschetta e Olive Piccante

Spicy Olives with Bruschetta

SERVES 4

450 g/1 lb black olives, stoned
 and finely chopped
2 sun-dried tomatoes in olive oil,
 drained and thinly sliced
1-2 red chillies, deseeded and
 finely chopped
grated rind of 2 lemons
extra virgin olive oil,
 for soaking and brushing
4 large slices sourdough bread or
 country bread, halved
2 garlic cloves, halved
4 spring onions, finely chopped
sea salt and pepper

1. Combine the olives, tomatoes, chillies and lemon rind in a non-metallic bowl. Season to taste with pepper, pour in enough oil to come almost to the top of the bowl, stir well and set aside for at least 1 hour for the flavours to blend, or for up to 1 week in a covered jar in the refrigerator.

2. When ready to serve, heat a ridged griddle pan over a very high heat. Working in batches, add as many pieces of bread as will fit in the pan in a single layer and chargrill for 3 minutes on each side, until marked with black lines and toasted. Alternatively, grill under a hot grill until toasted.

3. Remove the bread slices from the pan and rub with the garlic halves, pressing down firmly, then brush with oil and sprinkle with salt. Set aside while you chargrill the remaining bread.

4. Cut each piece of toast into thirds and put on a serving platter. Stir the spring onions into the olive mixture, then spoon the mixture into a serving bowl and serve with the pieces of toast.

Funghi Farciti
Creamy Stuffed Mushrooms

SERVES 4

25 g/1 oz dried ceps
225 g/8 oz floury potatoes,
   diced
2 tbsp melted butter
4 tbsp double cream
2 tbsp snipped fresh chives
8 portobello mushrooms
25 g/1 oz Emmenthal cheese,
   grated
150 ml/5 fl oz vegetable stock
salt and pepper

1. Preheat the oven to 220°C/425°F/Gas Mark 7. Place the dried ceps in a small bowl. Add enough boiling water to cover and leave to soak for 20 minutes.

2. Meanwhile, cook the potatoes in a saucepan of lightly salted boiling water for 10 minutes, until cooked through and tender. Drain well and mash until smooth.

3. Drain the soaked ceps and then chop them finely. Mix them into the mashed potatoes.

4. Thoroughly blend the butter, cream and chives together and pour into the potato mixture, mixing well. Season to taste with salt and pepper.

5. Remove the stalks from the portobello mushrooms. Chop the stalks and stir them into the potato mixture. Spoon the mixture into the mushrooms and sprinkle the cheese over the top.

6. Arrange the stuffed mushrooms in a shallow baking dish and pour in the stock.

7. Cover the dish and cook in the preheated oven for 20 minutes. Uncover and cook for a further 5 minutes, until golden. Serve the mushrooms immediately.

Insalata di Crudo, Salami & Fichi

Ham & Salami Salad with Figs

1. Trim the stems of the figs to leave just a short length, then cut the figs into quarters.

2. Arrange the ham and salami on a large serving platter.

3. Wash and dry the herbs and rocket and put in a bowl with the prepared figs.

4. Whisk the lemon juice and oil together in a small bowl and season well with salt and pepper. Pour the lemon juice and oil mixture into the bowl with the herbs, rocket and figs. Toss carefully until all the ingredients are well coated in the dressing.

5. Spoon the figs and salad on top of the meat on the serving platter. Serve immediately.

SERVES 6

6 ripe figs
6 thin slices prosciutto
12 thin slices salami
1 small bunch of fresh
  basil, separated into
  small sprigs
a few fresh mint sprigs
handful of rocket leaves
2 tbsp lemon juice
4 tbsp extra virgin
  olive oil
salt and pepper

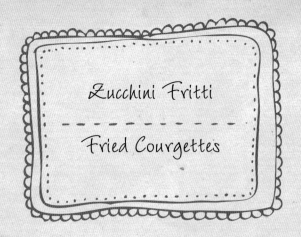

Zucchini Fritti

Fried Courgettes

SERVES 4

2 tbsp olive oil, plus extra
   for drizzling
1 onion, finely chopped
2 large garlic cloves,
   finely chopped
400 g/14 oz courgettes, halved
   lengthways and thinly sliced
½ tsp dried oregano
150 ml/5 fl oz passata
salt and pepper
Italian bread slices, to serve
   (optional)

1. Heat the oil in a large frying pan over a medium heat. Add the onion, reduce the heat to low and fry, stirring, for 5—8 minutes, until it is just starting to turn a pale golden colour. Stir in the garlic.

2. Add the courgettes and oregano and season to taste with salt and pepper. Increase the heat to medium—high and fry, turning over the courgette slices occasionally, for 5—8 minutes, until just starting to become tender.

3. Add the passata, bring to the boil and cook, without stirring, until the courgettes are tender but not mushy. Adjust the seasoning, if necessary.

4. Transfer the courgettes to a warmed serving dish and drizzle with a little oil. Set aside to cool and serve with slices of bread (if using).

Minestrone
Minestrone

SERVES 6

2 tbsp olive oil
1 large onion, chopped
2 garlic cloves, finely chopped
2 celery sticks, chopped
½ small white cabbage, shredded
150 ml/5 fl oz red wine
1.7 litres/3 pints vegetable stock
55 g/2 oz dried cannellini
beans, soaked overnight
and drained
4 plum tomatoes, peeled,
deseeded and chopped
2 tbsp tomato purée
2 tsp sugar
2 carrots, diced
55 g/2 oz fresh shelled peas
55 g/2 oz French beans,
cut into short lengths
55 g/2 oz dried soup pasta
2 tbsp chopped fresh mixed herbs
salt and pepper
grated Parmesan cheese, to serve

1. Heat the oil in a large saucepan. Add the onion, garlic and celery and cook over a low heat, stirring occasionally, for 5—7 minutes, until the onion has softened. Stir in the cabbage and cook, stirring frequently, for a further 5 minutes.

2 Increase the heat to medium, pour in the wine and cook for about 2 minutes, until the alcohol has evaporated, then pour in the stock. Add the cannellini beans and bring to the boil, then reduce the heat, cover and simmer for 2½ hours.

3. Add the tomatoes, tomato purée, sugar, carrots, peas, French beans, pasta and herbs and season to taste with salt and pepper. Simmer for 20—25 minutes, until the pasta is cooked and the vegetables are tender.

4. Ladle the soup into warmed bowls and serve immediately with Parmesan cheese.

Tortelloni in Brodo

- - - - - - - - - -

Pasta in Chicken Soup

1. Put the chicken, bay leaves, carrot, celery, onion and 2 teaspoons of salt into a large stockpot or deep saucepan. Pour in the water to cover and slowly bring to just below boiling point, skimming the surface occasionally to remove the scum. Do not allow the liquid to boil.

2. Reduce the heat to low, cover and leave to simmer for 1 hour. Skim the surface again, if necessary. Stir in the cheese rind, re-cover and simmer for a further 20 minutes, or until the chicken is tender and the juices run clear when a skewer is inserted into the thickest part of the meat. Remove the chicken pieces (and set aside if using for the main course, see Mama's Tip on right). Remove and discard the cheese rind.

3. Strain the liquid into a large bowl, pressing down on the vegetables. Skim the surface, then transfer 1.2 litres/2 pints of the broth to a large saucepan. Adjust the salt, if necessary, and add pepper to taste.

4. Bring to the boil, add the tortelloni and cook for 2 minutes, or according to the packet instructions, until they are al dente.

5. Ladle the pasta and broth into bowls and serve with Parmesan cheese for sprinkling (if using).

SERVES 4

1 oven-ready chicken, about
   1.6 kg/3 lb 8 oz, cut into
   pieces and skinned
2 bay leaves
1 large carrot, roughly chopped
1 large celery stick with
   leaves, roughly chopped
1 large onion, unpeeled,
   cut into quarters
2 litres/3½ pints water
5-cm/2-inch piece Parmesan
   cheese rind
300 g/10½ oz fresh tortelloni
salt and pepper
freshly grated Parmesan cheese,
   to serve (optional)

Mamá's Tip:
Canny Italian cooks turn this simple dish
into a two-course meal. Keep the chicken
hot and serve it as the main course.

Zuppa di Pomodoro

Fresh Tomato Soup with Pasta

SERVES 4

1 tbsp olive oil
4 large plum tomatoes
1 onion, cut into quarters
1 garlic clove, thinly sliced
1 celery stick, roughly chopped
500 ml/18 fl oz chicken stock
55 g/2 oz dried soup pasta
salt and pepper
chopped fresh flat-leaf parsley,
    to garnish

1. Pour the oil into a large, heavy-based saucepan and add the tomatoes, onion, garlic and celery. Cover and cook over a low heat, occasionally shaking gently, for 45 minutes, until pulpy.

2. Transfer the mixture to a food processor or blender and process to a smooth purée.

3. Push the purée through a sieve into a clean saucepan.

4. Add the stock and bring to the boil. Add the pasta, bring back to the boil and cook for 8—10 minutes, or according to the packet instructions, until the pasta is tender but still firm to the bite. Season to taste with salt and pepper.

5. Ladle into warmed bowls, sprinkle with parsley and serve immediately.

Zuppa di Vongole
Clam Soup

1. Heat the oil in a large saucepan over a medium heat. Add the fish heads, onion, carrot, celery and fennel, reduce the heat to low and simmer for 8 minutes. Add the garlic and simmer for a further 2 minutes.

2. Stir in the wine, bring to the boil and boil until reduced by half. Add the passata, water and chilli flakes (if using), and season with salt and pepper. Bring to the boil, skimming the surface occasionally, then reduce the heat to low, cover and simmer for 15 minutes.

3. Meanwhile, rinse the clams in several changes of water until the water runs clear. Discard any with broken shells and any that refuse to close when tapped. Preheat the grill to high and toast the bread on both sides.

SERVES 4

4 tbsp olive oil
2 fish heads or 350–400 g/
  12–14 oz fish trimmings
1 onion, chopped
1 carrot, finely diced
1 celery stick, finely diced
1 fennel bulb, finely diced
2 large garlic cloves, chopped
250 ml/9 fl oz dry white wine
700 ml/1¼ pints passata
700 ml/1¼ pints water
pinch of chilli flakes
  (optional)
1.3 kg/3 lb scrubbed live clams
4 slices day-old Italian bread
500 g/1 lb 2 oz tomatoes,
  deseeded and diced
1 tbsp finely chopped
  fresh mint
1 tbsp finely chopped
  fresh dill
salt and pepper

4. Strain the soup through a sieve lined with muslin, pressing down to extract as much flavour as possible. Transfer the strained liquid to a large saucepan and bring to the boil over a high heat. Reduce the heat to low, add the clams, cover and simmer for 3—5 minutes, until the clams have opened. Use a slotted spoon to remove and discard any clams that remain closed.

5. Stir in the tomatoes, mint and dill and adjust the seasoning, if necessary. Simmer for a further 2 minutes. Place a piece of bread in the base of four warmed bowls, then ladle over the clams and soup. Serve immediately.

Caponata
Italian Aubergines

Mama's Tip:
Caponata improves if kept in the refrigerator for a couple of days and is a great dish to take on a picnic.

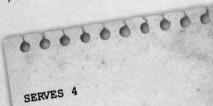

SERVES 4

4 tbsp olive oil
2 celery sticks, chopped
2 red onions, chopped
450 g/1 lb aubergines, diced
1 garlic clove, finely
   chopped
5 plum tomatoes, chopped
3 tbsp red wine vinegar
1 tbsp sugar
3 tbsp stoned green olives
2 tbsp capers
4 tbsp chopped fresh
   flat-leaf parsley
salt and pepper
ciabatta bread, to serve

1. Heat half of the oil in a large, heavy-based saucepan. Add the celery and onions and cook over a low heat, stirring occasionally, for 5 minutes, until softened but not coloured.

2. Add the remaining oil and the aubergines. Cook, stirring frequently, for about 5 minutes, until the aubergine starts to colour.

3. Add the garlic, tomatoes, vinegar and sugar and mix well. Cover the mixture with a circle of greaseproof paper and simmer gently for about 10 minutes.

4. Remove the greaseproof paper, stir in the olives and capers and season to taste with salt and pepper. Pour into a serving dish and set aside to cool to room temperature.

5. When cool, sprinkle over the parsley. Serve immediately with ciabatta bread.

VENEZIA
ST MARK'S BASILICA

Perfetto Pizza & Pasta

Ahh, perfetto pizza and pasta — the staple dishes of any Italian family cook! This is simple, wholesome and delicious food, suitable for all ages, all walks of life and for all times of the day. If the humblest peasant sweating in the vineyards of Calabria can sit down to Mushroom Pizza or Home-Made Gnocchi & Walnut Pesto, then so can Il Primo Ministro and the dignitaries of Rome! You know, it is a source of mystery to me why people ever buy frozen pizza. I hear from my son Gianluca, who wears a suit and works in the city, that for some people today modern life can be busy and fast paced. Apparently there is not always time to prepared home-cooked meals… to which I say *nonsenso!* As this chapter shows, creating *perfetto* pizza and pasta is something everyone can do with ease and enjoyment.

Pizza alle Salsiccie

Italian Sausage Pizza

1. Put the onion into a non-metallic bowl, sprinkle over 2 teaspoons of salt, toss and set aside for at least 20 minutes.

2. Meanwhile, preheat the oven to 220°C/425°F/Gas Mark 7. Dust two large baking sheets with polenta and set aside.

3. Heat the oil in a large frying pan over a high heat. Add the sausage meat and fry, stirring, for 3—5 minutes, until cooked through. Transfer to a sieve and leave to drain.

4. Rinse the onion, then pat completely dry with kitchen paper and set aside.

5. Turn out the dough onto a lightly floured work surface and gently knead. Divide into four equal pieces and roll each piece into a ball. Work with one ball at a time, keeping the remainder covered.

6. Using a lightly floured rolling pin, roll out each ball of dough into a 23—25-cm/9—10-inch round and transfer to a prepared baking sheet. Spread a quarter of the sauce over each round, then sprinkle with a quarter of the sausage meat and a quarter of the onion. Scatter a quarter of the cheese over each round and season with salt and pepper.

7. Bake the pizzas in the preheated oven for 15—18 minutes, until the crust is crisp and the cheese is melted and golden. Serve immediately.

1 red onion, thinly sliced
fine polenta or plain flour,
  for dusting
2 tbsp olive oil
500 g/1 lb 2 oz spicy or mild
  Italian sausages, skinned and
  coarsely crumbled
1 quantity Pizza Dough
  (see page 45)
Italian 00 flour or strong white
  flour, for kneading
125 ml/4 fl oz ready-made tomato
  pizza sauce
55 g/2 oz freshly grated
  Parmesan cheese
salt and pepper

Mamá's Tip:
For all my wisdom about how to create
the perfect pizza, read my advice on pages
44 and 45.

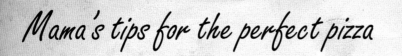

Nothing says Italian family food like pizza. I remember many summers ago my son Gianluca once tried to tell me we Italians actually took the recipe from the Ancient Greeks. To this, I replied that pizza has been cooked in Mama's family for hundreds of years — if anything the Ancient Greeks owe their food to my descendants and I don't care what the history books say!

And what's more, we've been making it the same way for pretty much all that time. Mama's basic pizza recipe is *molto facile* — and *molto delizioso*!

Mama's Basic Pizza Dough

MAKES FOUR 23–25–CM/9–10–INCH PIZZAS

450 g/1 lb Italian 00 or strong
  white flour, plus extra for
  dusting
7 g/¼ oz easy blend dried yeast
1 tsp salt
1 tbsp extra virgin olive oil,
  plus extra for the bowl
225–300 ml/8–10 fl oz water,
  heated to 46°C/115°F

1. Mix the flour, yeast and salt together in a large bowl and make a well in the centre. Add the oil and 225 ml/8 fl oz of water and gradually stir in the flour from the side until a soft dough forms — caress the flour in, firmly but gently, like you're bathing a *bambino*. Add more water, if needed, to create a soft dough.

2. Turn out the dough onto a lightly floured surface and knead until smooth and elastic. You can be a little firmer now — show the dough that Mama is boss! Once you're happy, shape the dough into a ball.

3. Wash and dry the bowl, then lightly run the inside with oil. Add the dough and roll it around so it is lightly coated. Cover the bowl with clingfilm and set aside in a warm place — Mama uses a corner of the kitchen, out of the sun but near the window — until the dough doubles in size, which can take up to 2 hours.

Use as directed in a recipe — but don't skimp on your toppings!

Pizza Fiorentina
Spinach & Olive Pizza

MAKES 2

fine polenta or plain flour,
    for dusting
250 g/9 oz spinach, washed and
    drained
½ quantity Pizza Dough (see
    page 45)
Italian 00 flour or strong white
    flour, for kneading
200 ml/7 fl oz ready-made tomato
    pizza sauce
2 garlic cloves, finely chopped
25 g/1 oz black olives, stoned
    and halved
2 tbsp garlic olive oil
2 eggs
85 g/3 oz finely grated Grana
    Padano cheese or Parmesan
    cheese
salt and pepper

1. Preheat the oven to 220°C/425°F/Gas Mark 7. Dust a large baking sheet with polenta and set aside.

2. Put the spinach into a small saucepan, place over a low heat and cook for 1—2 minutes, or until it has wilted. Drain the spinach through a sieve and press down with the back of a spoon to remove any remaining water.

3. Turn out the dough onto a lightly floured work surface and gently knead. Divide into two equal pieces and roll each piece into a ball. Work with one ball at a time, keeping the other covered.

4. Using a lightly floured rolling pin, roll out each ball of dough into a 23—25-cm/9—10-inch round and transfer to the prepared baking sheet. Spread half of the sauce over each round, then sprinkle each pizza with garlic. Top with the spinach and olives, drizzle over the garlic oil and season to taste.

5. Bake in the preheated oven for 11—13 minutes, then remove from the oven and make a small indentation in the centre of each pizza. Break an egg into each indentation and scatter over the cheese. Return to the oven and bake for a further 3—5 minutes, or until the eggs are just cooked and the bases are crisp. Serve immediately.

Pizza Margherita
Cheese & Tomato Pizza

1. Preheat the oven to 220°C/425°F/Gas Mark 7. Dust a large baking sheet with polenta and set aside.

2. Turn out the dough onto a lightly floured work surface and gently knead. Divide into two equal pieces and roll each piece into a ball. Work with one ball at a time, keeping the other covered.

3. Using a lightly floured rolling pin, roll out each ball of dough into a 23—25-cm/9—10-inch round and transfer to the prepared baking sheet.

4. Top each pizza round with the tomato and mozzarella slices. Season to taste with salt and pepper, sprinkle with the basil and drizzle with the oil.

5. Bake in the preheated oven for 15—18 minutes, or until the crust is crisp and the cheese is melted and golden.

6. Serve immediately.

MAKES 2

fine polenta or plain flour, for dusting
½ quantity Pizza Dough (see page 45)
Italian 00 flour or strong white flour, for kneading
6 tomatoes, thinly sliced
175 g/6 oz mozzarella cheese, thinly sliced
2 tbsp shredded fresh basil
2 tbsp olive oil
salt and pepper

Pizza alle Verdure
- - - - - - - - - - - - -
Vegetable Pizza

1. Preheat a ridged griddle pan over a high heat. Brush the courgette slices with oil, then add as many as will fit in the pan in a single layer and chargrill for 1—2 minutes on each side, until marked with black lines and heated through. Set aside and repeat with the remaining slices.

2. Meanwhile, preheat the oven to 220°C/425°F/Gas Mark 7. Dust two large baking sheets with polenta and set aside.

3. Turn out the dough onto a lightly floured work surface and gently knead. Divide into four equal pieces and roll each piece into a ball. Work with one ball at a time, keeping the remainder covered.

4. Using a lightly floured rolling pin, roll out each ball of dough into a 23—25-cm/9—10-inch round and transfer to a prepared baking sheet.

MAKES 4

2 courgettes, halved
    lengthways and thinly sliced
    into half-moon shapes
1 tbsp olive oil, plus extra
    if needed
fine polenta or plain flour,
    for dusting
1 quantity Pizza Dough
    (see page 45)
Italian 00 flour or strong
    white flour, for kneading
125 ml/4 fl oz ready-made
    tomato pizza sauce
16 sun-dried tomatoes in oil,
    drained and quartered
2 tsp dried dill
115 g/4 oz soft goat's
    cheese, crumbled
salt and pepper

Mama's Tip:
Scatter over a handful of stoned
black olives before cooking the
pizza - they are a perfect pairing
with the goat's cheese.

5. Spread a quarter of the sauce over each round, then add a quarter
of the courgette slices, a quarter of the tomatoes and a quarter of the
dill. Scatter a quarter of the cheese over each round and season with salt
and pepper.

6. Bake the pizzas in the preheated oven for 15—18 minutes, until the
crust is crisp and the cheese is melted and golden. Serve immediately.

Pizza ai Gamberi
Seafood Pizza

MAKES 2

fine polenta or plain flour,
  for dusting
½ quantity Pizza Dough (see
  page 45)
Italian 00 flour or strong
  white flour, for kneading
200 ml/7 fl oz ready-made
  tomato pizza sauce
200 g/7 oz canned tuna
140 g/5 oz cooked prawns
100 g/3½ oz mozzarella
  cheese, grated
1 tbsp chopped fresh parsley
1 tbsp chopped fresh oregano
1 garlic clove, chopped
2 tbsp. olive oil

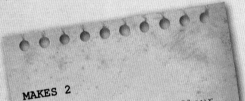

1. Preheat the oven to 220°C/425°F/Gas Mark 7. Dust a large baking sheet with polenta and set aside.

2. Turn out the dough onto a lightly floured work surface and gently knead. Divide into two equal pieces and roll each piece into a ball. Work with one ball at a time, keeping the other covered.

3. Using a lightly floured rolling pin, roll out each ball of dough into a 23—25-cm/9—10-inch round and transfer to the prepared baking sheet.

4. Top each pizza round with the tomato sauce. Roughly flake the tuna and spread it over each pizza, then arrange the prawns on top. Sprinkle with the mozzarella.

5. Mix together the parsley, oregano, garlic and olive oil, and drizzle the mixture over the pizzas.

6. Bake in the preheated oven for about 15—18 minutes, or until the crust is crisp and the cheese is melted and golden. Serve immediately.

Calzone ai Tonno e Peperoni Rossi
Tuna & Red Pepper Calzone

MAKES 4

fine polenta or plain flour,
   for dusting
1 quantity Pizza Dough
   (see page 45)
Italian 00 flour or strong white
   flour, for kneading
125 ml/4 fl oz ready-made tomato
   pizza sauce
350 g/12 oz canned tuna in olive
   oil, drained and flaked
12 chargrilled red peppers in
   olive oil, drained and sliced,
   oil reserved
100 g/3½ oz black olives, stoned
   and sliced
salt and pepper

1. Preheat the oven to 220°C/425°F/Gas Mark 7. Dust a large baking sheet with polenta and set aside.

2. Turn out the dough onto a lightly floured work surface and gently knead. Divide into four equal pieces and roll each piece into a ball. Work with one ball at a time, keeping the remainder covered.

3. Using a lightly floured rolling pin, roll each ball of dough into a 23—25-cm/9—10-inch round. Spread a quarter of the sauce over half of the round, leaving a 1-cm/ ½ -inch border. Add a quarter of the tuna, then top with a quarter of the red peppers and a quarter of the olives. Season to taste with salt and pepper.

4. Fold the uncovered half of the dough over the filling and securely fold the edge in on itself. Take care to make the fold tight, so the calzone doesn't split while baking, allowing the filling to seep out.

5. Gently transfer the calzone to the prepared baking sheet and cover with a teatowel while you prepare the remaining calzones.

6. Lightly brush the tops of the calzones with some of the reserved oil from the peppers. Bake in the preheated oven for 15—18 minutes, until puffed and golden brown. Leave to cool for a few minutes, then serve.

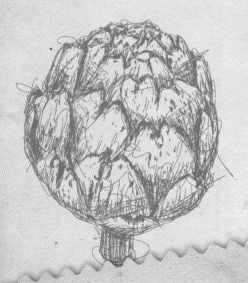

Pizza Capricciosa

- -

Capricciosa Pizza

1. Preheat the oven to 220°C/425°F/Gas Mark 7. Dust a large baking sheet with polenta and set aside.

2. Turn out the dough onto a lightly floured work surface and gently knead. Divide into two equal pieces and roll each piece into a ball. Work with one ball at a time, keeping the other covered.

3. Using a lightly floured rolling pin, roll out each ball of dough into a 23—25-cm/9—10-inch round and transfer to the prepared baking sheet.

4. Top each pizza round with the tomato sauce, spreading almost to the edges. Scatter over the salami, orange pepper, artichoke hearts and oregano, then top with the cheese. Season to taste with salt and pepper.

5. Bake in the preheated oven for 15—18 minutes, or until the crust is crisp and the cheese is melted and golden. Serve immediately.

MAKES 2

fine polenta or plain flour, for dusting
½ quantity Pizza Dough (see page 45)
Italian 00 flour or strong white flour, for kneading
200 ml/7 fl oz ready-made tomato pizza sauce
250 g/9 oz Italian salami, thinly sliced
1 orange pepper, deseeded and finely sliced
150 g/5½ oz artichoke hearts in vegetable oil, drained and cut into quarters
½ tsp dried oregano
175 g/6 oz soft goat's cheese, thinly sliced
salt and pepper

Pizza ai Funghi

Mushroom Pizza

1. Preheat the oven to 220°C/425°F/Gas Mark 7. Dust two large baking sheets with polenta and set aside.

2. Heat the oil in a large frying pan over a medium—high heat. Add the mushrooms, thyme and chilli flakes (if using). Sprinkle with salt and fry, stirring, for 5—8 minutes, until the mushrooms are tender and reabsorb the liquid they give off.

3. Turn out the dough onto a lightly floured work surface and gently knead. Divide into four equal pieces and roll each piece into a ball. Work with one ball at a time, keeping the remainder covered.

4. Using a lightly floured rolling pin, roll each ball of dough into a 23—25-cm/9—10-inch round and transfer to a prepared baking sheet. Using a slotted spoon, transfer a quarter of the mushroom mixture to each pizza, draining off as much oil as possible. Spread out to cover the surface. Scatter over the cheese and season to taste with salt and pepper.

5. Bake in the preheated oven for 15—18 minutes, until the crust is crisp and the cheese is melted and golden. Serve immediately.

MAKES 4

fine polenta or plain flour,
    for dusting
2 tbsp olive oil
800 g/1 lb 12 oz field
    mushrooms, thinly sliced
leaves from 4 fresh thyme
    sprigs, or 1 tbsp dried thyme
½ tsp dried chilli flakes
    (optional)
1 quantity Pizza Dough
    (see page 45)
Italian 00 flour or strong white
    flour, for kneading
350 g/12 oz Taleggio cheese,
    rinded and thinly sliced
salt and pepper

Mama's Tip:
For a delicious garlic flavour, use
garlic oil to fry the mushrooms and
drizzle some over the pizza once it is
cooked.

Pizza ai Carciofi

Artichoke Pizza

MAKES 4

fine polenta or plain flour,
   for dusting
1 quantity Pizza Dough
   (see page 45)
Italian 00 flour or strong white
   flour, for kneading
400 g/14 oz artichoke hearts
   in oil
8 mild whole chillies in oil
4 garlic cloves, finely chopped
2 tbsp finely chopped fresh
   flat-leaf parsley
4 tbsp olive oil
200 g/7 oz mozzarella cheese,
   diced
salt and pepper

1. Preheat the oven to 220°C/425°F/Gas Mark 7. Dust two large baking sheets with polenta and set aside.

2. Turn out the dough onto a lightly floured work surface and gently knead. Divide into four equal pieces and roll each piece into a ball. Work with one ball at a time, keeping the remainder covered.

3. Using a lightly floured rolling pin, roll out each ball of dough into a 23—25-cm/9—10-inch round and transfer to a prepared baking sheet.

4. Slice the artichoke hearts lengthways. Sprinkle the artichokes and chillies on top of each pizza round. Sprinkle with garlic and half of the parsley. Season with salt and pepper and drizzle on the olive oil. Put the mozzarella on top of the pizzas and bake for about 15—18 minutes. Sprinkle with the remaining parsley before serving.

rosso

Ziti al Forno
Baked Ziti

1. Preheat the oven to 220°C/425°F/Gas Mark 7 and lightly grease a large baking dish with oil.

2. Bring a large saucepan of lightly salted water to the boil. Add the ziti, bring back to the boil and cook for 2 minutes less than specified in the packet instructions.

3. Meanwhile, beat together the ricotta cheese, half of the mozzarella cheese and a third of the Parmesan cheese in a large bowl. Season with salt and pepper and set aside.

4. Just before the pasta finishes cooking, take 4 tablespoons of the pasta cooking liquid and beat into the cheese mixture until a creamy sauce starts to form.

5. Drain the pasta, add it to the bowl and stir until coated with cheese. Stir in the tomato sauce, parsley and chilli flakes (if using), and stir until well mixed.

6. Tip the pasta into the prepared baking dish and smooth the surface. Sprinkle over the remaining mozzarella cheese and Parmesan cheese.

7. Place the dish on a baking sheet and bake in the preheated oven for 25–30 minutes, until golden brown on top. Leave to stand for a few minutes, then serve straight from the dish.

SERVES 4

olive oil, for greasing
350 g/12 oz dried ziti
   or penne
250 g/9 oz ricotta cheese
250 g/9 oz mozzarella cheese,
   grated
85 g/3 oz freshly grated
   Parmesan cheese
700 ml/1¼ pints ready-made
   tomato sauce with herbs
2 tbsp chopped fresh parsley
pinch of dried chilli flakes
   (optional)
salt and pepper

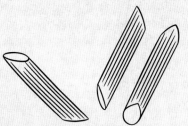

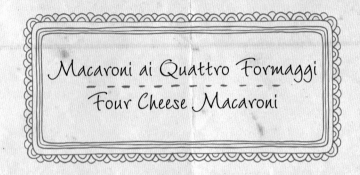

Macaroni ai Quattro Formaggi
Four Cheese Macaroni

1. Preheat the oven to 200°C/400°F/Gas Mark 6. Lightly grease a large baking dish with butter, then set aside. Mix a third of the Parmesan cheese with the breadcrumbs and set aside.

2. Bring a large saucepan of lightly salted water to the boil, add the macaroni, bring back to the boil and cook for 2 minutes less than specified in the packet instructions. Drain well, rinse with cold water, drain again and set aside.

3. Meanwhile, melt the butter in a saucepan over a medium heat. Sprinkle over the flour and stir for 2 minutes, until blended. Remove the pan from the heat and stir in the milk, stirring constantly to prevent lumps forming.

85 g/3 oz freshly grated
  Parmesan cheese
55 g/2 oz fine dry breadcrumbs
400 g/14 oz dried macaroni
40 g/1½ oz butter, plus extra
  for greasing
40 g/1½ oz plain flour
450 ml/16 fl oz lukewarm milk
freshly grated nutmeg,
  to taste
85 g/3 oz dolcelatte cheese,
  finely chopped
85 g/3 oz provolone or
  Taleggio cheese, grated
55 g/2 oz mozzarella cheese,
  diced
olive oil, for drizzling
salt and pepper

4. Return the pan to the heat, stir in the nutmeg and season with salt and pepper. Slowly bring to the boil, stirring, until the sauce thickens. Stir in the remaining Parmesan cheese, the dolcelatte cheese and the provolone cheese and continue stirring until the cheese melts and is blended. Stir in the mozzarella cheese.

5. Add the macaroni and stir to coat in the sauce. Adjust the seasoning, if necessary. Tip the mixture into the prepared dish and smooth the surface. Sprinkle the breadcrumb mixture over the top and drizzle with oil.

6. Place the dish on a baking sheet and bake in the preheated oven for 20—25 minutes, until golden brown on top. Leave to stand for a few minutes, then serve straight from the dish.

Ravioli Classici
Classic Ravioli

1. To make the filling, put the breadcrumbs and milk into a bowl and set aside to soak. Roll the dough into eight balls and wrap in clingfilm.

2. Heat the oil in a large frying pan over a medium heat. Add the shallot and stir for 1—2 minutes, or until beginning to soften. Stir in the beef, pork, garlic, ham and sage and season with salt and pepper. Stir for a further 2—4 minutes, breaking up the meat until it is brown all over. Stir in the breadcrumbs. Add the wine, bring to the boil and boil, stirring, until it has just evaporated. Stir in the cheese.

3. Lightly dust a work surface and a baking sheet with semolina. Roll one dough ball into a strip about 10 cm/4 inches wide and 50 cm/ 20 inches long, as described on page 67, and lay it on the work surface.

4. Use a 7.5-cm/3-inch round cutter to cut out 6—8 rounds. Place 1 teaspoon of filling slightly off centre on each. Rub water around the edge of each round, then gently fold over the top half and press to seal. Use the tines of a fork to press all around.

5. Transfer to the prepared baking sheet and cover. Repeat with the remaining dough, re-rolling the trimmings, until all the filling has been used. Leave to rest for at least 1 hour or cover and chill for up to 24 hours.

6. Bring a large saucepan of lightly salted water to the boil, add the ravioli, bring back to the boil and cook for 2 minutes, until tender. Use a slotted spoon to transfer the ravioli to a warmed serving dish. Drizzle with oil and sprinkle with salt and pepper. Serve with Parmesan cheese.

SERVES 4

1 quantity Pasta Dough, rested
 but not rolled,(see page 66)
fine semolina, for dusting
olive oil,to serve
salt and pepper

FILLING

15 g/½ oz fresh white
 breadcrumbs
1 tbsp milk
1 tbsp olive oil
1 shallot, very finely chopped
85 g/3 oz fresh beef mince
85 g/3 oz fresh pork mince
2 garlic cloves,
 finely chopped
2 slices Parma ham,
 finely chopped
½ tsp dried sage or thyme
4 tbsp red wine
30 g/1 oz finely grated
 Parmesan cheese,
 plus extra to serve
salt and pepper

Mama's Tip:
For advice on making your own
pasta dough, see pages 66 and 67.

Now I am going to teach you my basic ravioli dough recipe. Lucky for you, it's molto facile!

MAKES ENOUGH FOR 4

200 g/7 oz Italian 00 or plain white flour, plus extra for kneading and dusting
½ tsp salt
2 eggs, beaten
2 tsp olive oil
fine semolina, for dusting

Mama's Basic Ravioli Dough

1. Sift the flour and salt together into a large bowl, then make a well in the centre. Add the eggs and oil and gradually stir together with a fork until the liquid has been absorbed. Use your hands to knead the dough in the bowl, firmly and gently, sprinkling in water, if necessary, until a dough forms.

2. Turn out the dough onto a lightly floured surface and knead until it becomes smooth and elastic. Shape the dough into a ball.

3. Wash and dry the bowl. Add the ball of dough, cover with clingfilm and leave to rest for at least 30 minutes.

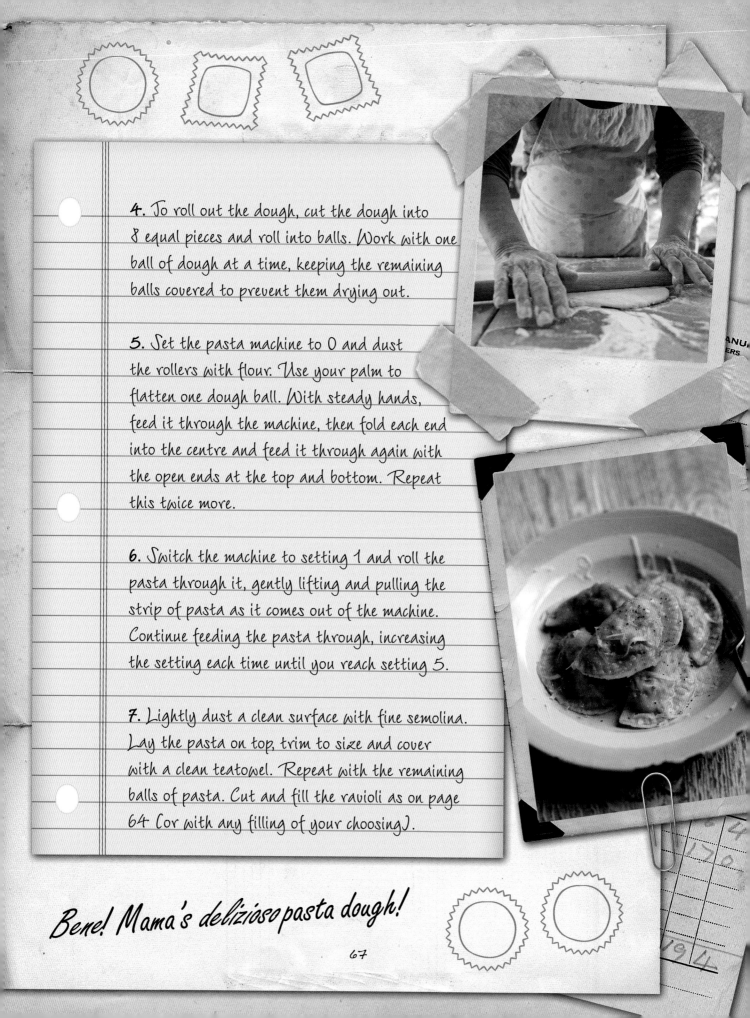

4. To roll out the dough, cut the dough into 8 equal pieces and roll into balls. Work with one ball of dough at a time, keeping the remaining balls covered to prevent them drying out.

5. Set the pasta machine to 0 and dust the rollers with flour. Use your palm to flatten one dough ball. With steady hands, feed it through the machine, then fold each end into the centre and feed it through again with the open ends at the top and bottom. Repeat this twice more.

6. Switch the machine to setting 1 and roll the pasta through it, gently lifting and pulling the strip of pasta as it comes out of the machine. Continue feeding the pasta through, increasing the setting each time until you reach setting 5.

7. Lightly dust a clean surface with fine semolina. Lay the pasta on top, trim to size and cover with a clean teatowel. Repeat with the remaining balls of pasta. Cut and fill the ravioli as on page 64 (or with any filling of your choosing).

Bene! Mama's delizioso pasta dough!

Lasagne ai Pollo & Funghi

Chicken & Mushroom Lasagne

1. Preheat the oven to 190°C/375°F/Gas Mark 5. For the white sauce, heat the milk, butter, flour and bay leaf in a saucepan over a low heat, whisking constantly, until smooth and thick. Season to taste with salt and pepper, cover and leave to stand.

2. Heat the oil in a large saucepan over a medium heat and fry the onion, stirring, for 3—4 minutes.

3. Add the chicken and pancetta and cook for 6—8 minutes. Stir in both types of mushrooms and cook for a further 2—3 minutes.

4. Add the wine and bring to the boil. Pour in the tomatoes, cover and simmer for 20 minutes. Stir in the basil.

5. Meanwhile, bring a large saucepan of lightly salted water to the boil. Add the lasagne sheets, bring back to the boil and cook for 8—10 minutes or according to the packet instructions. Drain well on a clean teatowel.

6. Spoon a third of the meat sauce into a large baking dish. Remove and discard the bay leaf from the white sauce. Spoon a quarter of the white sauce over the meat sauce. Arrange three of the lasagne sheets over the white sauce. Repeat the layers twice more, finishing with a layer of white sauce.

7. Sprinkle with the Parmesan and bake in the preheated oven for 35—40 minutes, until the topping is golden brown and bubbling. Serve immediately.

SERVES 4

2 tbsp olive oil
1 large onion, finely chopped
500 g/1 lb 2 oz fresh chicken
   mince
100 g/3½ oz pancetta, chopped
250 g/9 oz chestnut mushrooms,
   chopped
100 g/3½ oz dried porcini
   mushrooms, soaked
150 ml/5 fl oz dry white wine
400 g/14 oz canned chopped
   tomatoes
3 tbsp chopped fresh basil
9 sheets dried lasagne
3 tbsp finely grated Parmesan
   cheese

WHITE SAUCE

600 ml/1 pint milk
55 g/2 oz butter
55 g/2 oz plain flour
1 bay leaf
salt and pepper

Mama's Tip:
If you find it hard to buy chicken mince,
you can either make your own by putting
some chicken meat in a food processor
or buy turkey mince instead.

3

6

7

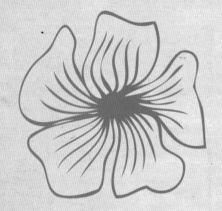

Linguine alla Puttanesca
Anchovy Linguine

1. Heat the oil in a heavy-based saucepan. Add the garlic and cook over a low heat, stirring frequently, for 2 minutes. Mash the anchovies to a pulp with a fork and add them to the pan.

2. Add the olives, capers and tomatoes and season to taste with cayenne pepper. Cover and simmer for 25 minutes.

3. Meanwhile, bring a saucepan of lightly salted water to the boil. Add the pasta, bring back to the boil and cook for 8—10 minutes, until tender but still firm to the bite.

4. Drain the pasta and transfer to a warmed serving dish. Spoon the anchovy sauce into the dish and toss the pasta, using two large forks, until well coated. Garnish with parsley and serve immediately.

SERVES 4

3 tbsp olive oil
2 garlic cloves, finely chopped
10 anchovy fillets, chopped
140 g/5 oz black olives, stoned and chopped
1 tbsp capers
450 g/1 lb plum tomatoes, peeled, deseeded and chopped
cayenne pepper, to taste
400 g/14 oz dried linguine
salt
2 tbsp chopped fresh flat-leaf parsley, to garnish

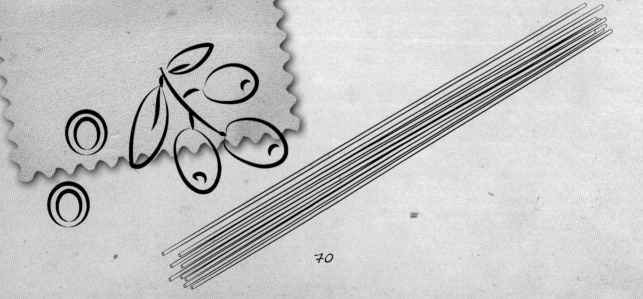

Fettucine Alfredo

Fettucine Alfredo

SERVES 4

400 g/14 oz dried fettucine
85 g/3 oz unsalted butter, diced
2 garlic cloves, finely chopped
400 ml/14 fl oz double cream
175 g/6 oz freshly grated
Parmesan cheese, plus extra to
serve (optional)
salt and pepper

1. Bring a large saucepan of lightly salted water to the boil. Add the pasta, bring back to the boil and cook for 8—10 minutes, until tender but still firm to the bite.

2. Meanwhile, melt the butter in a large frying pan over a medium heat. Add the garlic and stir for 1 minute, taking care that it doesn't brown. Stir in the cream and bring to the boil. Add half of the cheese and stir until melted, then reduce the heat to very low and season to taste with salt and pepper.

3. Drain the pasta without shaking and reserve a little of the cooking liquid. Immediately add the hot pasta and the remaining cheese to the cream sauce, using two forks to toss until well coated. If the sauce seems too thick, add a little of the reserved cooking liquid to thin it, then toss again.

4. Divide between warmed bowls and serve immediately, with extra cheese (if using).

Rigatoni ai Zucchini
Roast Courgette Rigatoni

SERVES 4

4 courgettes, chopped
2½ tbsp olive oil
1 onion, finely chopped
1 garlic clove, crushed
800 g/1 lb 12 oz canned
    chopped tomatoes
6 sun-dried tomatoes, chopped
225 ml/8 fl oz vegetable stock
½ tsp dried oregano
280 g/10 oz dried rigatoni
125 g/4½ oz mascarpone cheese
salt and pepper
large handful of fresh basil
    leaves, torn into pieces

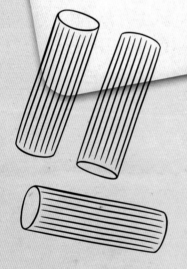

1. Preheat the oven to 200°C/400°F/Gas Mark 6. Place the courgettes and 1½ tablespoons of the oil in a large baking dish. Toss together and spread out in a single layer. Roast in the preheated oven for 15—20 minutes until tender and lightly browned.

2. Meanwhile, heat the remaining oil in a saucepan. Add the onion and garlic and cook over a low heat for 5 minutes until soft. Add the canned tomatoes, sun-dried tomatoes, stock and oregano. Simmer for 10 minutes until the liquid has reduced slightly.

3. Bring a large saucepan of lightly salted water to the boil. Add the rigatoni, bring back to the boil and cook for 8—10 minutes, or until tender but still firm to the bite. Drain well, then return to the pan.

4. Add the mascarpone cheese to the hot sauce and stir until melted and smooth. Season well with salt and pepper. Add to the pasta with the roasted courgettes and the basil leaves. Toss together until the pasta is well coated in sauce. Serve immediately.

Penne al Pollo

Creamy Chicken Penne

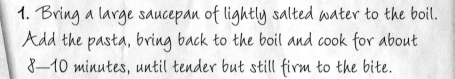

SERVES 2

200 g/7 oz dried penne
1 tbsp olive oil
2 skinless, boneless chicken
   breasts
4 tbsp dry white wine
115 g/4 oz frozen peas
5 tbsp double cream
salt
4–5 tbsp chopped fresh flat-leaf
   parsley, to garnish

1. Bring a large saucepan of lightly salted water to the boil. Add the pasta, bring back to the boil and cook for about 8—10 minutes, until tender but still firm to the bite.

2. Meanwhile, heat the oil in a frying pan. Add the chicken and cook over a medium heat for about 4 minutes on each side.

3. Pour in the wine and cook over a high heat until it has almost evaporated.

4. Drain the pasta. Add the peas, cream and pasta to the frying pan and stir well. Cover and simmer for 2 minutes.

5. Garnish the chicken and pasta mixture with parsley and serve immediately.

Mama's Tip:
Add a ¼ teaspoon of crushed dried chillies with 400 g/14 oz of canned tomatoes to give a little more depth to the sauce.

bianco

**Cannelloni di Spinaci
e Ricotta**

**Spinach & Ricotta
Cannelloni**

1. Preheat the oven to 180°C/350°F/Gas Mark 4. Grease a large baking dish with the melted butter.

2. Bring a large saucepan of lightly salted water to the boil. Add the cannelloni tubes, bring back to the boil and cook for 6—8 minutes, until nearly tender. Drain and rinse, then spread out on a clean teatowel.

3. For the filling, put the spinach and ricotta into a food processor and process briefly until combined. Add the egg and pecorino and process to a smooth paste. Transfer to a bowl, add the nutmeg and season to taste with salt and pepper.

4. Spoon the filling into a piping bag fitted with a 1-cm/½-inch nozzle. Carefully open a cannelloni tube and pipe in a little of the filling. Place the filled tube in the prepared dish and repeat.

5. For the cheese sauce, melt the butter in a saucepan. Add the flour to the butter and cook over a low heat, stirring constantly, for 1 minute.

6. Remove from the heat and gradually stir in the hot milk. Return to the heat and bring to the boil, stirring constantly. Simmer over a low heat, stirring frequently, for 10 minutes, until thickened and smooth.

7. Remove from the heat, stir in the Gruyère and season to taste with salt and pepper.

8. Spoon the cheese sauce over the filled cannelloni. Cover the dish with foil and bake in the preheated oven for 20—25 minutes. Serve immediately.

SERVES 4

melted butter, for greasing
12 dried cannelloni tubes,
   each about 7.5 cm/
   3 inches long
salt and pepper

FILLING
140 g/5 oz frozen spinach,
   thawed and drained
115 g/4 oz ricotta cheese
1 egg
3 tbsp grated pecorino cheese
pinch of freshly grated nutmeg

CHEESE SAUCE
25 g/1 oz butter
2 tbsp plain flour
600 ml/1 pint hot milk
85 g/3 oz Gruyère cheese,
   grated

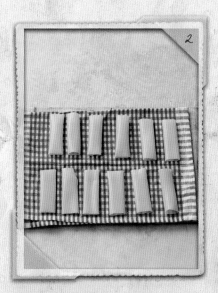

Gnocchi con Tacchino & Broccoli
Turkey & Broccoli Gnocchi

SERVES 4

1 tbsp sunflower oil
500 g/1 lb 2 oz turkey
    strips
2 small leeks, sliced diagonally
500 g/1 lb 2 oz ready-made fresh
    gnocchi
200 g/7 oz broccoli, cut into
    bite-sized pieces
85 g/3 oz crème fraîche
1 tbsp wholegrain mustard
3 tbsp orange juice
salt and pepper
3 tbsp toasted pine nuts,
    to serve

1. Heat the oil in a large frying pan. Add the turkey and leeks and fry over a high heat for 5—6 minutes.

2. Meanwhile, bring a saucepan of lightly salted water to the boil. Add the gnocchi and broccoli, then cook for 3—4 minutes.

3. Drain the gnocchi and broccoli and stir into the turkey mixture.

4. Mix together the crème fraîche, mustard and orange juice in a small bowl. Season to taste with salt and pepper, then stir into the pan. Serve immediately, sprinkled with pine nuts.

Gnocchi con Sugo di Noce
Home-made Gnocchi & Walnut Pesto

1. Cook the potatoes in their skins in a large saucepan of boiling water for 30—35 minutes, until tender. Drain well and leave to cool slightly.

2. Meanwhile, put all of the pesto ingredients in a food processor or blender and process for 2 minutes.

3. When the potatoes are cool enough to handle, peel off their skins and pass the flesh through a sieve into a large bowl or press through a potato ricer. Season well with salt and pepper and add the Parmesan. Beat in the egg and sift in the flour.

4. Lightly mix together, then turn out onto a lightly floured work surface. Knead lightly to form a smooth dough. If it is too sticky, add a little more flour.

5. Roll out the dough into a long log. Cut into 2.5-cm/1-inch pieces and press with a fork to give the traditional ridged effect. Transfer to a floured baking sheet and cover with a teatowel.

6. Bring a large saucepan of water to the boil, add the gnocchi and cook for 1—2 minutes. Remove with a slotted spoon and serve immediately with the walnut pesto.

SERVES 4

450 g/1 lb floury potatoes
55 g/2 oz freshly grated Parmesan cheese
1 egg, beaten
200 g/7 oz plain flour, plus extra for dusting
salt and pepper

WALNUT PESTO
40 g/1½ oz fresh flat-leaf parsley leaves
2 tbsp capers
2 garlic cloves, crushed
175 ml/6 fl oz extra virgin olive oil
70 g/2½ oz chopped walnuts
40 g/1½ oz freshly grated pecorino or Parmesan cheese

Splendido Suppers

Supper at Casa di Mama is always an event. Even the simplest meals are a family affair, a coming together at the end of the day to give thanks for all we have — even if sometimes it can seem like all we have is each other. There are some evenings where I'm simply putting together the simplest frittata for myself and Alberto. On other evenings, I could be preparing a hearty vegetable stew for Marco, Filippo, their wives and *bambini*, or even celebrating a visit by the *nipoti* and *pronipoti* with something extra special, like Baked Oregano Lobster. Whatever the occasion, suppers are the heart and soul of the family cook. It is at supper — this most everyday of meals — that a family cook shows what she is really made of. And I should know: I've raised a family of 40 on Mama's suppers, after all!

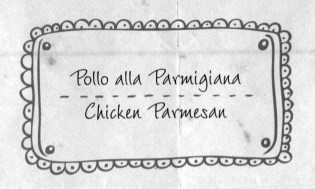

Pollo alla Parmigiana
Chicken Parmesan

1. To make the sauce, heat the oil in a large saucepan. Add the onion and fry, stirring, for 2 minutes. Add the garlic and cook, stirring, until the onion is soft. Stir in the mixed herbs, tomatoes, passata, oregano and sugar and season to taste. Bring to the boil, then cover and simmer for 15 minutes. Transfer to a blender or food processor and purée.

2. Meanwhile, preheat the oven to 200°C/400°F/Gas Mark 6. Spread the flour over a plate. Beat the eggs in a wide bowl, and put the breadcrumbs on another plate. Halve the chicken breasts horizontally.

3. Place the chicken pieces between sheets of clingfilm and pound with a meat mallet or rolling pin until about 5 mm/ 1/4 inch thick. Season both sides with salt and pepper. Dust a chicken breast with flour, shaking off the excess, then dip in the egg to coat. Dip in the breadcrumbs to coat both sides, then set aside and repeat with the remaining chicken pieces.

4. Heat the oil in a frying pan over a medium—high heat. Add as many chicken pieces as will fit in the pan in a single layer and fry on each side for 2 minutes, until golden. Drain on kitchen paper. Fry the remaining pieces, adding extra oil, if necessary. Pour half of the sauce into a baking dish that will hold the chicken in a single layer. Arrange the chicken on top, then pour over the remaining sauce. Arrange the mozzarella on top and sprinkle over the Parmesan cheese. Bake in the preheated oven for 20—25 minutes, or until the cheese is melted, golden and bubbling. Leave to stand for 5 minutes, then garnish with parsley and serve immediately.

SERVES 4

100 g/3½ oz plain flour
2 eggs
200 g/7 oz dry breadcrumbs
4 skinless, boneless chicken
  breasts, 250 g/9 oz each
2 tbsp olive oil, plus extra
250 g/9 oz mozzarella, sliced
125 g/4½ oz grated Parmesan
salt and pepper
chopped fresh flat-leaf
  parsley, to garnish

SIMPLE MARINARA SAUCE

2 tbsp olive oil
1 large onion, chopped
2 large garlic cloves, chopped
1 tbsp dried mixed herbs
800 g/1 lb 12 oz canned
  chopped tomatoes
250 ml/9 fl oz passata
2 tsp dried oregano
pinch of sugar
salt and pepper

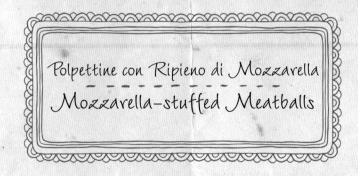

Polpettine con Ripieno di Mozzarella
Mozzarella-stuffed Meatballs

1. Mix together the breadcrumbs and milk in a bowl and set aside while you assemble the other ingredients.

2. Put the beef, Parmesan cheese, garlic, egg, grated onion, parsley, basil, mixed herbs, and salt and pepper to taste in a bowl. Add the breadcrumb mixture and use your hands to mix together.

3. Wet your hands and shape the mixture into 12 equal-sized balls. Use your finger to make an indentation in the centre of each ball, push in a cube of mozzarella cheese and re-roll the meat into a smooth ball. Do make sure the join is sealed, so that the melting cheese doesn't leak out during cooking. At this point the meatballs can be covered and chilled for up to 12 hours. Return to room temperature before frying.

SERVES 4

85 g/3 oz fine dry breadcrumbs
2 tbsp milk
600 g/1 lb 5 oz fresh beef mince
125 g/4½ oz finely grated
  Parmesan cheese, plus extra
  for serving
2 large garlic cloves,
  finely chopped
1 egg, beaten
3 onions, 1 grated and
  2 thinly sliced
2 tbsp finely chopped fresh
  flat-leaf parsley
1 tbsp finely chopped fresh
  basil, plus extra to garnish
1 tsp dried mixed herbs
100 g/3½ oz mozzarella, cut
  into 12 x 1-cm/½-inch cubes
2 tbsp olive oil, plus extra
  for frying
500 ml/18 fl oz passata
pinch of sugar
salt and pepper

4. Heat a thin layer of oil in a large frying pan. Add as many meatballs as will fit in the pan and fry for 3—5 minutes, until brown all over. Set aside and keep warm while cooking the remaining meatballs.

5. Heat 2 tablespoons of oil in a large saucepan or casserole dish. Stir in the sliced onions, reduce the heat to low and fry, stirring, for 5—8 minutes, until golden brown. Add the passata and sugar and season with salt and pepper. Stir in the meatballs.

6. Bring to the boil, then reduce the heat, cover and simmer for 20—25 minutes, or until the meatballs are cooked through when you cut one open. Adjust the seasoning of the sauce, if necessary. Serve immediately on warmed plates, sprinkled with Parmesan cheese.

Mama's guide to setting an Italian dinner table

In Apulia we don't stand on ceremony. I hear that in countries like England dinners are molto formale affairs, with many strict rules about which fork to use and when, which way the port must be passed... Not at Mama's table!

Mama believes a big family meal should, most of all, be an enjoyable experience — what is the point otherwise? If everyone is worried about breaking some silly rule of etiquette, nobody relaxes... and if nobody relaxes, nobody has a good time.

You need some rules, of course: Mama insists on everyone sitting to eat, and once you're seated at my table, you follow the law of my table — but don't worry. My rules are made to enhance the experience, not stifle it!

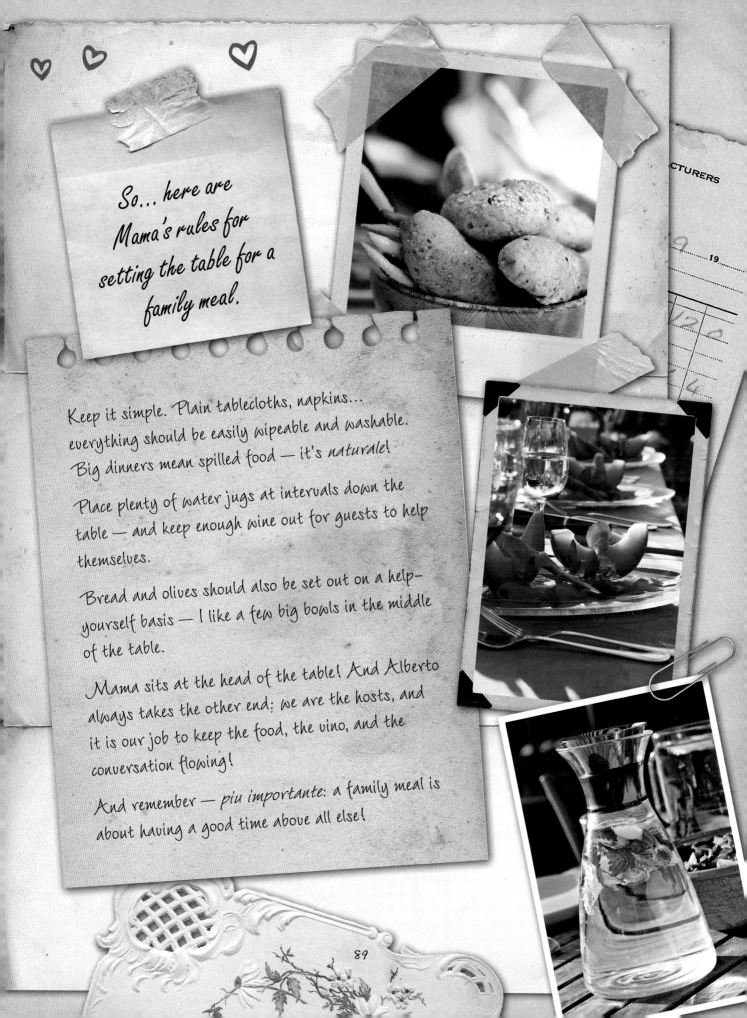

So... here are Mama's rules for setting the table for a family meal.

Keep it simple. Plain tablecloths, napkins... everything should be easily wipeable and washable. Big dinners mean spilled food — it's *naturale!*

Place plenty of water jugs at intervals down the table — and keep enough wine out for guests to help themselves.

Bread and olives should also be set out on a help-yourself basis — I like a few big bowls in the middle of the table.

Mama sits at the head of the table! And Alberto always takes the other end: we are the hosts, and it is our job to keep the food, the vino, and the conversation flowing!

And remember — *piu importante*: a family meal is about having a good time above all else!

89

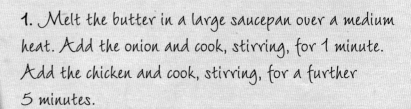

Risotto con Pollo
Chicken Risotto

SERVES 4

55 g/2 oz butter
1 onion, chopped
125 g/4½ oz skinless, boneless
    chicken breasts, chopped
350 g/12 oz risotto rice
1 tsp ground turmeric
300 ml/10 fl oz dry white wine
1.2 litres/2 pints chicken stock,
    plus extra if needed
75 g/2¾ oz chestnut mushrooms,
    sliced
50 g/1¾ oz cashew nuts, halved
salt and pepper
Parmesan cheese shavings and
    fresh basil leaves,
    to garnish

1. Melt the butter in a large saucepan over a medium heat. Add the onion and cook, stirring, for 1 minute. Add the chicken and cook, stirring, for a further 5 minutes.

2. Add the rice and stir over a medium heat for 1 minute, without browning. Add the turmeric and mix well.

3. Gradually stir in the wine, then stir in the stock, a ladleful at a time, waiting for each ladleful to be absorbed before stirring in the next.

4. Simmer for 20 minutes, stirring from time to time, until the rice is tender and nearly all of the liquid has been absorbed. If necessary, add a little more stock to prevent the risotto from drying out.

5. Stir in the mushrooms and cashew nuts, and cook for a further 3 minutes. Season to taste with salt and pepper.

6. Remove from the heat and spoon it into warmed serving dishes. Scatter over the Parmesan shavings and basil leaves and serve immediately.

Risotto con Verdure
Vegetable Risotto

1. Heat the butter and olive oil in a large saucepan and fry the onion, stirring, for 3—4 minutes, until softened.

2. Add the rice and stir over a medium heat for 1 minute, without browning.

3. Add the wine and boil rapidly, stirring, until almost all evaporated.

4. Stir the stock into the pan a ladleful at a time, allowing each ladleful to be absorbed before adding more.

5. After 15 minutes, add the asparagus and continue cooking, adding stock when necessary.

6. After a further 5 minutes, stir in the walnuts and lemon rind, then adjust the seasoning, adding salt and pepper to taste.

7. Remove from the heat and drizzle over a little walnut oil, if using, stirring in lightly. Spoon the risotto into warmed serving dishes and serve immediately, garnished with strips of lemon zest.

SERVES 4

15 g/½ oz butter
3 tbsp olive oil
1 small onion, finely chopped
350 g/12 oz risotto rice
150 ml/5 fl oz dry white wine
1.5 litres/2¾ pints vegetable stock
200 g/7 oz asparagus tips, cut into 6-cm/2½-inch lengths
40 g/1½ oz chopped walnuts
grated rind of 1 lemon
salt and pepper
walnut oil, to serve (optional)
strips of lemon zest, to garnish

Rollatini

Aubergine Rollatini

1. Preheat the oven to 230°C/450°F/Gas Mark 8. Place the aubergine slices in a single layer on a baking sheet, lightly brush with oil and sprinkle with salt and pepper.

2. Place in the preheated oven and bake for 8—10 minutes, until tender. Remove from the oven and set aside. Reduce the oven temperature to 220°C/425°F/Gas Mark 7.

3. Spread a thin layer of sauce in the base of a baking dish large enough to hold eight aubergine rolls in a single layer, then set aside.

4. Put the ricotta cheese, goat's cheese, basil and lemon rind in a bowl. Season with salt and pepper and beat together until smooth. Add the egg and beat until incorporated.

5. Place an aubergine slice on the work surface. Place 2—3 teaspoons of filling at one end, then gently roll the aubergine lengthways around the filling. Place in the prepared dish, seam side down. Continue until all the aubergine slices and filling have been used.

6. Pour the remaining sauce over the aubergine rolls and scatter with the mozzarella cheese. Place the dish on a baking sheet and bake for 25—30 minutes, until the filling is set and the cheese is golden brown. Leave to stand for 5 minutes, then serve.

SERVES 4

1 large aubergine, sliced
  lengthways into 8 slices
2 tbsp olive oil
½ quantity Simple Marinara
  Sauce (see page 85), or
  500 ml/18 fl oz ready-made
  tomato and basil pasta sauce
100 g/3½ oz ricotta cheese
55 g/2 oz soft goat's cheese,
  rind removed, crumbled
4 tbsp finely shredded basil
  leaves
finely grated rind of 1 lemon
1 large egg, beaten
125 g/4½ oz mozzarella cheese,
  coarsely grated
salt and pepper

Mama's Tip:
*A little freshly grated nutmeg added to
the filling will turn this dish into a taste
sensation!*

Pollo alla Cacciatora

Chicken Cacciatora

SERVES 4

1 chicken, weighing 1.5 kg/3 lb
  5 oz, cut into 6 or 8 pieces
125 g/4½ oz plain flour
3 tbsp olive oil
150 ml/5 fl oz dry white wine
1 green pepper, deseeded and sliced
1 red pepper, deseeded and sliced
1 carrot, finely chopped
1 celery stick, finely chopped
1 garlic clove, crushed
200 g/7 oz canned chopped tomatoes
salt and pepper
fresh flat-leaf parsley sprigs,
  to garnish

1. Lightly dust the chicken pieces with the flour. Heat the oil in a large frying pan. Add the chicken and cook over a medium heat until browned all over. Remove from the pan and set aside.

2. Drain off all but 2 tablespoons of the fat in the pan. Add the wine and simmer, stirring, for a few minutes. Stir in the peppers, carrot, celery and garlic, season to taste with salt and pepper and simmer for about 15 minutes.

3. Add the browned chicken and tomatoes to the pan. Cover and simmer, stirring frequently, for 30 minutes, until the chicken is tender and the juices run clear when a skewer is inserted into the thickest part of the meat.

4. Taste and adjust the seasoning, adding salt and pepper if needed. Transfer to warmed bowls, garnish with parsley sprigs and serve immediately.

Salsiccie & Peperoni
Sausage & Peppers

SERVES 4

4 tbsp olive oil
8 Italian sausages
1 large green pepper,
    deseeded and sliced
1 large red pepper, deseeded
    and sliced
2 onions, sliced
2 large garlic cloves,
    finely chopped
150 ml/5 fl oz passata
salt and pepper
basil leaves, to garnish

1. Heat the oil in a large frying pan with a tight-fitting lid over a medium heat. Add the sausages, in batches if necessary, and fry, stirring, until brown all over. Remove from the pan and set aside. Pour off all but 2 tablespoons of the fat from the pan.

2. Add the green pepper, red pepper and onion to the pan and cook, stirring, for 3 minutes, until beginning to soften. Add the garlic and stir for a further 1 minute.

3. Add the passata and season to taste with salt and pepper. Return the sausages to the pan and bring the mixture to the boil, stirring.

4. Reduce the heat to very low, cover and simmer for 12—15 minutes, until the sausages are cooked through and the peppers are tender. Adjust the seasoning, if necessary. Garnish with basil leaves and serve immediately. Alternatively, transfer to a bowl, leave to cool completely and serve as a cold starter for eight people.

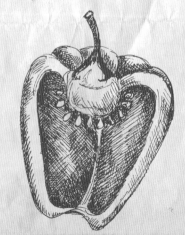

Stufato di Verdure

Italian Vegetable Stew

SERVES 4

4 garlic cloves, finely chopped
1 small acorn squash, diced
1 red onion, sliced
2 leeks, sliced
1 aubergine, sliced
1 small celeriac, diced
2 turnips, sliced
2 plum tomatoes, chopped
1 carrot, sliced
1 courgette, sliced
2 red peppers, deseeded and sliced
1 fennel bulb, sliced
175 g/6 oz chard
2 bay leaves
½ tsp fennel seeds
½ tsp chilli powder
pinch of each dried thyme,
   dried oregano and sugar
25 g/1 oz fresh basil leaves, torn
125 ml/4 fl oz olive oil
225 ml/8 fl oz vegetable stock
4 tbsp chopped fresh parsley
salt and pepper
2 tbsp freshly grated Parmesan
   cheese, to serve

1. Put the garlic and squash in a large heavy-based saucepan with all the other vegetables, the bay leaves, fennel seeds, chilli powder, thyme, oregano, sugar and half of the basil.

2. Pour the oil and stock into the saucepan. Mix all the ingredients together well, then bring to the boil.

3. Reduce the heat, cover and simmer for 30 minutes, or until all the vegetables are tender. Discard the bay leaves.

4. Sprinkle in the remaining basil and the parsley and season to taste with salt and pepper. Serve immediately, sprinkled with the Parmesan.

Filetti di Tacchino
Italian Turkey Steaks

SERVES 4

1 tbsp olive oil
4 turkey escalopes or steaks
2 red peppers, deseeded
   and sliced
1 red onion, sliced
2 garlic cloves, finely chopped
300 ml/10 fl oz passata
150 ml/5 fl oz medium white wine
1 tbsp chopped fresh marjoram
400 g/14 oz canned cannellini
   beans, drained and rinsed
3 tbsp fresh white breadcrumbs
salt and pepper
fresh basil sprigs, to garnish

1. Heat the oil in a flameproof casserole, add the turkey and cook over a medium heat for 5—10 minutes, turning occasionally, until browned all over. Transfer to a plate using a slotted spoon.

2. Add the red peppers and onion to the casserole and cook over a low heat, stirring occasionally, for 5 minutes, or until softened. Add the garlic and cook for a further 2 minutes.

3. Return the turkey to the casserole and add the passata, wine and marjoram. Season to taste with salt and pepper. Bring to the boil, then reduce the heat, cover and simmer, stirring occasionally, for 25—30 minutes, or until the turkey is cooked through and the juices run clear when a skewer is inserted into the thickest part of the meat. Meanwhile, preheat the grill to medium.

4. Stir the cannellini beans into the casserole and simmer for a further 5 minutes. Sprinkle the breadcrumbs over the top and place under the preheated grill for 2—3 minutes, or until golden. Serve immediately, garnished with basil sprigs.

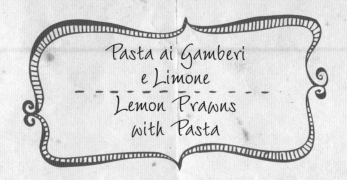

Pasta ai Gamberi
e Limone
Lemon Prawns
with Pasta

1. Melt the butter with the oil in a large frying pan over a medium—high heat. Add the shallots, garlic and chilli flakes (if using), and fry for 1—2 minutes, until the shallots are soft but not brown.

2. Stir in the lemon rind, wine and lemon juice, bring to the boil and cook, stirring occasionally, for 2—3 minutes, until the sauce reduces slightly and the flavours blend. If the butter starts to brown, immediately remove the pan from the heat.

3. Reduce the heat, add the prawns and cook, stirring occasionally, for 2—3 minutes, until they turn pink and curl. Stir in the parsley and season with salt and pepper.

4. Meanwhile, bring a large saucepan of lightly salted water to the boil. Add the pasta, bring back to the boil and cook for 2—4 minutes, or according to the packet instructions. Drain the pasta well, then immediately add it to the pan with the prawns, using two forks to mix and blend all the ingredients together.

5. Divide the pasta and prawns between warmed bowls, pour the cooking juices over and serve immediately.

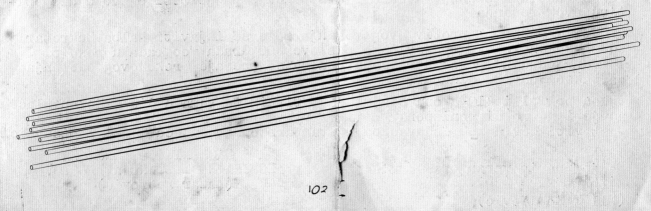

SERVES 4

125 g/4½ oz butter
125 ml/4 fl oz olive oil
2 shallots, finely chopped
6 garlic cloves, finely chopped
¼ tsp dried red chilli flakes
   (optional)
finely grated rind of
   1 large lemon
85 ml/3 fl oz dry white wine
2 tbsp lemon juice
600 g/1 lb 5 oz jumbo prawns,
   peeled and deveined
2 tbsp finely chopped fresh
   flat-leaf parsley
350 g/12 oz dried angel
   hair pasta
salt and pepper

Mama's Tip:
This recipe is also great with spaghetti,
linguine or tagliatelle - just use
whichever you have left in the cupboard!

Frittata Primavera
Spring Vegetable Frittata

SERVES 2

15 g/½ oz pine nuts
5 eggs
55 g/2 oz fine asparagus
  spears
55 g/2 oz French beans
55 g/2 oz fresh shelled
  baby broad beans or peas
1 tsp olive oil
10 g/¼ oz butter
25 g/1 oz fresh Parmesan
  cheese shavings
handful of rocket leaves
salt and pepper
crusty bread, to serve

1. Toast the pine nuts in a large, heavy-based frying pan with a heatproof handle over a medium heat, stirring until they are golden brown. Tip out onto a plate.

2. Using a fork, lightly beat the eggs in a bowl with salt and pepper to taste.

3. Preheat the grill to high. Half-fill the frying pan with water and bring to the boil. Add the asparagus, French beans and broad beans. Simmer for 2 minutes, then drain.

4. Dry the pan and return to a medium heat. Add the oil and butter and, when melted and foaming, add the vegetables and pour the beaten eggs over the top.

5. Cook the frittata for 1–2 minutes, until lightly browned underneath, then place the pan under the preheated grill and cook for 1–2 minutes, until just set in the middle.

6. Pile the Parmesan cheese shavings and rocket on top of the frittata and scatter with the pine nuts. Serve immediately with crusty bread.

Polenta con Ragù di Funghi
Polenta with Mushroom Ragù

1. To make the ragù, strain the ceps through a sieve lined with muslin or through a coffee filter, then set the liquid aside. Rinse and slice the ceps and set them aside.

2. Heat the oil and butter in a large frying pan with a lid over a medium heat. Add the wild mushrooms and fry, stirring, for 5 minutes. Stir in the ceps, garlic and rosemary and season with salt and pepper. Continue frying until the wild mushrooms have given off their liquid and reabsorbed it.

3. Add the vermouth and 125 ml/4 fl oz of the reserved strained liquid and bring to the boil, stirring. Reduce the heat to very low, cover the pan and simmer for 15—20 minutes until the mushrooms are very tender and the flavours blend. Adjust the seasoning, if necessary.

SERVES 4

500 g/1 lb 2 oz ready-made
   firm polenta, cut into
   12 x 1-cm/½-inch slices
garlic-flavoured olive oil
chopped fresh flat-leaf
   parsley, to garnish

MUSHROOM RAGÙ

30 g/1 oz dried ceps, soaked
   in at least 175 ml/6 fl oz
   hot water for at least
   30 minutes
3 tbsp extra virgin olive oil
30 g/1 oz butter
800 g/1 lb 12 oz mixed wild
   mushrooms, thickly sliced
4 garlic cloves,
   finely chopped
1 tsp dried rosemary or thyme
4 tbsp red vermouth
salt and pepper

4. Meanwhile, preheat a ridged griddle pan over a high heat and preheat the oven to 180°C/350°F/Gas Mark 4. Brush the polenta slices with oil, add as many to the pan as will fit in a single layer and chargrill for 3 minutes on each side, until marked with black lines and heated through. Transfer the cooked polenta slices to the oven to keep warm while you chargrill the remainder.

5. Arrange the polenta slices on warmed plates and spoon the ragù over. Garnish with parsley and serve immediately.

Risotto con Polpettine Piccante

Spicy Meatball Risotto

SERVES 4

1 thick slice white bread
water or milk, for soaking
450 g/1 lb fresh pork mince
2 garlic cloves, finely chopped
1 tbsp finely chopped onion
1 tsp black peppercorns, crushed
pinch of salt
1 egg
corn oil, for shallow-frying
400 g/14 oz canned chopped
    tomatoes
1 tbsp tomato purée
1 tsp dried oregano
1 tsp fennel seeds
pinch of sugar
1 tbsp olive oil
40 g/1½ oz butter
1 small onion, finely chopped
280 g/10 oz risotto rice
150 ml/5 fl oz red wine
1 litre/1¾ pints beef stock
salt and pepper
fresh basil leaves, to garnish

1. Place the bread into a bowl, add the water and leave to soak for 5 minutes. Squeeze out the water and place into a bowl with the pork, garlic, onion, peppercorns and salt. Add the egg and mix thoroughly. Shape the mixture into 12 equal balls. Heat the corn oil in a frying pan. Add the meatballs and fry thoroughly. Remove and drain.

2. Combine the tomatoes, purée, herbs and sugar in a large saucepan. Add the meatballs and bring to the boil. Reduce the heat and simmer for 30 minutes.

3. Heat the oil with 25 g/1 oz of the butter in a deep saucepan until the butter has melted. Add the onion and cook for 5 minutes, until golden. Reduce the heat, add the rice and mix to coat in the oil and butter. Cook, stirring constantly, for 2—3 minutes, or until the grains are translucent. Add the wine and cook, stirring constantly until reduced.

4. Gradually add the hot stock. Stir constantly and add more liquid as the rice absorbs each addition. Cook for 20 minutes. Season to taste. Lift out the cooked meatballs and add to the risotto. Remove the risotto from the heat and add the remaining butter. Mix well. Divide the risotto and meatballs between four warmed plates. Drizzle with the tomato sauce, garnish with the basil and serve immediately.

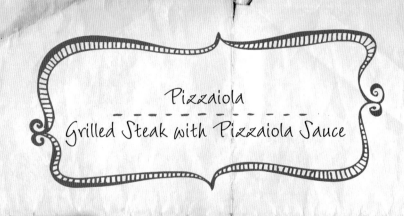

Pizzaiola
Grilled Steak with Pizzaiola Sauce

SERVES 4

3 tbsp olive oil, plus extra
   for brushing
700 g/1 lb 9 oz tomatoes,
   peeled and chopped
1 red pepper, deseeded
   and chopped
1 onion, chopped
2 garlic cloves, finely chopped
1 tbsp chopped fresh flat-leaf
   parsley
1 tsp dried oregano
1 tsp sugar
4 x 175 g/6 oz rump steaks
salt and pepper

1. Place the oil, tomatoes, pepper, onion, garlic, parsley, oregano and sugar in a heavy-based saucepan and season to taste with salt and pepper. Bring to the boil, lower the heat and simmer for 15 minutes.

2. Meanwhile, snip any fat around the outsides of the steaks. Season each generously with pepper (no salt) and brush with oil.

3. Preheat the grill to high. Cook the steaks under the preheated grill for 1 minute on each side. Lower the heat to medium and cook according to taste: 1½–2 minutes each side for rare; 2½–3 minutes each side for medium; and 3–4 minutes each side for well done.

4. Transfer the steaks to warmed individual plates and spoon over the sauce. Serve immediately.

Scaloppine alla Marsala
Veal Escalopes with Marsala

1. Put each veal escalope between two pieces of clingfilm or inside a polythene food bag and, using a rolling pin, gently beat out until 3 mm/⅛ inch thick.

2. Season the escalopes well with salt and pepper and dust with the flour.

3. Heat the oil in a large frying pan, add the escalopes and cook over a high heat for 1 minute on each side, or until lightly browned. Add the Marsala and leave the liquid to bubble around the escalopes for 1 minute.

4. Serve immediately with the pan juices poured over the meat. Garnish with parsley and serve accompanied by mashed potatoes or a green salad.

SERVES 4

4 veal escalopes, about
    70 g/2½ oz each
1 tbsp plain flour
3 tbsp olive oil
150 ml/5 fl oz Marsala
salt and pepper
handful of chopped fresh
    flat-leaf parsley, to garnish
mashed potatoes or green salad,
    to serve

Mama's Tip:
You can use skinned chicken breasts
instead of veal - prepare them in the
same way, following the instructions for
the veal.

Aragosta al Forno
Baked Oregano Lobster

1. Preheat the oven to 180°C/350°F/Gas Mark 4. Bring a kettle to the boil. Select a roasting tin that will hold the lobster tails upright.

2. Put a lobster tail, on a chopping board, shell down. Use a pair of scissors to cut lengthways through the shell without cutting through the tail fan and being careful not to crush the shell. Use a small knife to cut the tail meat in half lengthways without cutting through the shell. Use the scissors to cut away the tough cartilage on top of the shell. Use the tip of a knife to cut out the black intestinal vein and remove. Repeat with the remaining tails. Cover and refrigerate the tails until required.

3. Heat the oil in a small frying pan. Add the shallot and fry for 1—2 minutes, until golden. Add the garlic and stir for a further 1 minute, or until the shallot is soft. Stir in the breadcrumbs, oregano, lemon rind and parsley and season with salt and pepper.

4. Very lightly season inside the split tails, then place them in the roasting tin, using balls of foil to wedge them upright, if necessary. Divide the oregano mixture between the four split tails, lightly pressing it into the splits, but not packing it in, and covering half the tails. You might have a little left over, depending on the size of the tails. Drizzle with oil.

5. Add enough boiling water to the tin to come halfway up the sides of the tails, taking care not to get any water on the stuffing. Bake in the preheated oven for 20 minutes, until the flesh at the thickest part under the stuffing is white. Remove from the oven and serve immediately.

SERVES 4

4 frozen lobster tails, about
   175 g/6 oz each, thawed and
   patted dry
4 tbsp olive oil, plus extra
   for drizzling
1 large shallot, very finely
   chopped
2 garlic cloves, very finely
   chopped
6 tbsp fine dry breadcrumbs
2 tsp dried oregano
finely grated rind of 2 lemons
1 tbsp very finely chopped
   fresh flat-leaf parsley
salt and pepper

Tonno Condito
Marinated Tuna Steaks

1. To make the marinade, combine the oil, orange juice, black olives, green olives, tomatoes, red pepper, thyme and orange rind in a non-metallic bowl. Season with salt and pepper and set aside.

2. Heat a large, ridged griddle pan over a medium—high heat until a splash of water 'dances' on the surface. Brush one side of each tuna steak with oil, place it in the pan and season the top with salt and pepper. Cook for 2 minutes, then turn and cook on the other side for a further 2 minutes for rare, or up to 5 minutes for well done.

3. Transfer the tuna steaks to a deep serving dish that will hold them all in a single layer. Pour the marinade over the top of the tuna steaks and set aside to cool.

SERVES 4

4 tuna steaks, each about
    140 g/5 oz
2 tbsp olive oil, plus extra
1 fennel bulb, thinly sliced
salt and pepper
rocket leaves and crusty
    bread, to serve

MARINADE
125 ml/4 fl oz olive oil
2 tbsp orange juice
55 g/2 oz black olives, stoned
    and diced
55 g/2 oz green olives, stoned
    and diced
2 large tomatoes, peeled,
    deseeded and diced
1 large chargrilled red
    pepper, deseeded and sliced
leaves from 4 fresh thyme
    sprigs, or 2 tsp dried thyme
finely grated rind of 1 orange
salt and pepper

4. Meanwhile, brush the fennel slices with oil, then place them in the pan in a single layer and chargrill until lightly marked on both sides. Transfer to the bowl with the tuna, pushing them down into the marinade.

5. To serve, place the tuna steaks on plates and spoon the fennel, olives and tomatoes over, then add the marinade sauce. Top with the rocket leaves. Serve with plenty of bread for mopping up the delicious marinade sauce.

Saltimbocca
Pork Rolls

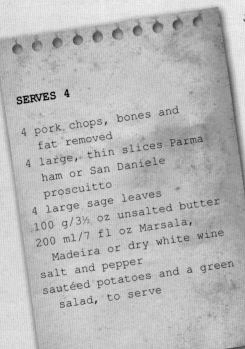

SERVES 4

4 pork chops, bones and
  fat removed
4 large, thin slices Parma
  ham or San Daniele
  proscuitto
4 large sage leaves
100 g/3½ oz unsalted butter
200 ml/7 fl oz Marsala,
  Madeira or dry white wine
salt and pepper
sautéed potatoes and a green
  salad, to serve

1. Lay the pork chops on a board and flatten them with a meat mallet or rolling pin until they are the same size as the ham slices. Lay down a piece of ham, put a piece of pork on top and place a sage leaf at the edge nearest to you.

2. Season with salt and pepper then roll the meat around the sage leaf and secure it with a cocktail stick. The ham should be on the outside. Repeat with all four chops.

3. Place a wide, heavy-based saucepan over a high heat. Add the butter and then the meat rolls and brown them quickly on all sides. Add the Marsala and reduce the heat to a simmer.

4. Cover and cook for about 10—15 minutes, until the meat is cooked through. The pork should not show any pink traces and the juices should run clear when pierced with a sharp knife or skewer.

5. Remove the rolls with a slotted spoon and keep them warm. Increase the heat and reduce the liquid for 2 minutes to thicken. Serve the rolls immediately with sautéed potatoes and a green salad and pour over a little of the sauce.

A good family get-together can involve people from three or four generations: when Mama has all her *bambini* home, my table will cater for old-timers like me and Alberto to my *pronipoti*, my beautiful great grandchildren.

A big family is a gift from heaven — but taking care of guests of all ages means a little planning might be needed...

Always include the *bambini*. In Apulia we say 'Nelle botti piccine ci sta il vino buono', or 'in the small barrels you find the good wine'. Why do some people insist on the little ones eating separately? With children at the table, there is always more joy.

Try to seat people where everyone can see everyone else — but keep parents near their *bambini*. The old like to see the energy of the young — but may not be so quick to deal with an unruly child.

Don't let your guests be lazy: at Casa di Mama everyone earns their dinner! Some help me in the kitchen, some choose the vino with Alberto. Others tell stories, sing songs or play games with the little ones. There should be no silence, no formality! This is a family dinner, remember, not high mass with Il Papa at the Vatican!

Celebrate the fact that you are all together — share in the wisdom of the old and the vigour of the young.

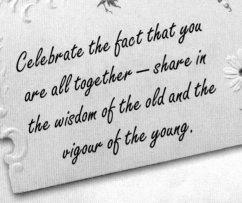

There is an Italian proverb: 'Chi mangia solo, crepa solo' — he who eats alone, dies alone. The best food tastes better in company: don't save your big gatherings for special occasions. Being alive and with people you love is cause enough for celebration.

Have something planned for after you have eaten. Games for the children, quieter time for the older guests. We all digest at our own pace.

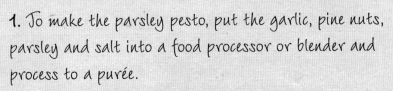

Filetti di Salmone con Pesto
Salmon Fillets with Pesto

SERVES 4

4 salmon steaks, about
  175 g/6 oz each
mixed salad and griddled
  ciabatta, to serve

PARSLEY PESTO
2 garlic cloves, roughly chopped
25 g/1 oz pine nuts
40 g/1½ oz fresh flat-leaf
  parsley, coarse stems removed
1 tsp salt
25 g/1 oz freshly grated
  Parmesan cheese
125 ml/4 fl oz extra virgin
  olive oil, plus extra
  if needed

1. To make the parsley pesto, put the garlic, pine nuts, parsley and salt into a food processor or blender and process to a purée.

2. Add the Parmesan and blend briefly again. Then add the olive oil and blend again. If the consistency is too thick, add some extra oil and blend again until smooth. Scrape into a bowl and set aside.

3. Meanwhile, preheat the grill to medium. Cook the salmon under the preheated grill for 10–15 minutes, depending on the thickness of the fillets, until the flesh turns pink and flakes easily.

4. Transfer the salmon to serving plates, top with the parsley pesto and serve immediately with salad and ciabatta.

bianco

Ribollita
Italian Cabbage & Bean Stew

1. Heat the olive oil in a large saucepan and cook the onions, carrots and celery over a medium heat, stirring frequently, for 10—15 minutes. Add the garlic, thyme, and season with salt and pepper to taste. Continue to cook for a further 1—2 minutes, until the vegetables are golden.

2. Add the cannellini beans to the pan and pour in the tomatoes. Add enough of the water to cover the vegetables.

3. Bring to the boil, then reduce the heat and simmer for 20 minutes. Add the parsley and cavolo nero and cook for a further 5 minutes.

4. Stir in the bread and add a little more water, if needed. The consistency should be thick.

5. Taste and adjust the seasoning, adding salt and pepper if needed. Serve immediately, drizzled with extra virgin olive oil.

SERVES 4

3 tbsp olive oil
2 red onions, roughly chopped
3 carrots, sliced
3 celery sticks, roughly chopped
3 garlic cloves, chopped
1 tbsp chopped fresh thyme
400 g/14 oz canned cannellini beans, drained and rinsed
400 g/14 oz canned chopped tomatoes
about 600 ml/1 pint water or vegetable stock
2 tbsp chopped fresh parsley
500 g/1 lb 2 oz cavolo nero or Savoy cabbage, cored and sliced
1 small day-old ciabatta loaf, torn into pieces
salt and pepper
extra virgin olive oil, to serve

Superbo Sides & Salads

Do you want to know what marks out the maestro from the rest of the crowd? What elevates the artist to genius? *Attenzione ai dettagli* — attention to detail. Sure, you can learn your steaks, your stews, your escalopes — but man cannot live on meat alone! And Mama cannot feed a family with meals lacking the trimmings, the extras, and all the *attenzione ai dettagli* that keep them coming back for more every day. Don't neglect your sides, and your salads! Doing so is the mark of the amateur cook! And, if they are properly done with the freshest vegetables, the crunchiest leaves or the sweetest herbs, a good Spinach in Gorgonzola, Carpaccio Salad or even Mama-style Roast Potatoes can be as beautiful a thing as you will see on any Italian family dinner table!

Peperoni & Cipolle

Slow-cooked Peppers & Onions

1. Heat the oil in a large frying pan with a tight-fitting lid over a medium heat. Stir in the onion, cover, reduce the heat to low and simmer for 8–10 minutes, until the onion is soft but not brown.

2. Stir in the mixed peppers and garlic and season to taste with salt and pepper. Re-cover the pan and simmer for 5 minutes. Stir in the tomatoes and thyme and bring to the boil, stirring.

3. Reduce the heat to very low (use a heat diffuser if you have one), re-cover the pan and leave to simmer for 20 minutes, until the peppers are tender. If the sauce is too runny, uncover and boil until it reaches the desired consistency. Adjust the seasoning, if necessary.

4. Spoon into a serving dish and serve hot or at room temperature.

SERVES 4

3 tbsp olive oil
1 large onion, thinly sliced
3 mixed peppers, such as red,
   orange and yellow, deseeded and
   cut into strips
2 garlic cloves, finely chopped
400 g/14 oz canned chopped tomatoes
2 tsp dried thyme
salt and pepper

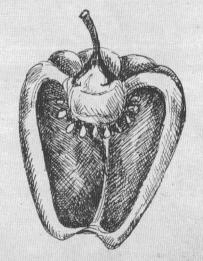

Cime di Rapa Gratinate

Broccoli Rabe Gratin

1. To make the sauce, put the milk, bay leaves and onion into a small saucepan with a pinch of salt and bring to simmering point. Remove from the heat, cover and leave to stand for at least 1 hour for the flavours to blend. Strain the milk and set aside.

2. Melt the butter in a saucepan over a medium—high heat. Add the flour and stir for 2 minutes, until it is blended and a paste forms. Remove the pan from the heat and gradually add the milk, stirring constantly, until it is blended and the sauce is smooth. Return to the heat and bring to just below boiling point, then reduce the heat and simmer for 5 minutes. Season with salt and pepper and set aside.

3. Meanwhile, preheat the grill to high and position the grill rack about 5 cm/2 inches below the heat. Bring a large saucepan of lightly salted water to the boil.

SERVES 4

750 g/1 lb 10 oz broccoli rabe
30 g/1 oz freshly grated
  Parmesan cheese
salt and pepper

BÉCHAMEL SAUCE
300 ml/10 fl oz milk
2 bay leaves
½ onion, studded with 4 cloves
30 g/1 oz butter, plus extra
  for greasing
2 tbsp Italian 00 flour or
  plain flour
salt and pepper

4. Remove and discard the thick bases of the broccoli stalks and any yellow leaves. Separate the thin stalks with leaves from the thick stalks with flower heads. Rinse the broccoli well in several changes of cold water.

5. Add the thick stalks with flower heads to the boiling water and boil for 2 minutes. Then add the thin stalks and boil for 6—8 minutes, until all the stalks are tender. Drain well, squeezing out any excess moisture.

6. Grease a shallow baking dish. Spread the broccoli rabe over the base of the dish and season with salt and pepper. Pour over the sauce and sprinkle over the cheese.

7. Place the dish under the preheated grill and cook for 10—12 minutes, until the top is bubbling and golden. Leave to stand for 2 minutes before serving.

Spinaci in Gorgonzola
Spinach in Gorgonzola Sauce

Mama's Tip:
This is even more delicious if you stir in a handful of toasted pine nuts just before serving.

SERVES 4

1 kg/2 lb 4 oz spinach
60 g/2¼ oz butter
½ tsp freshly grated nutmeg
125 ml/4 fl oz dry white wine
125 ml/4 fl oz milk
125 g/4½ oz Gorgonzola
    cheese, crumbled
2 egg yolks
salt and pepper

bianca

1. Remove and discard any tough stems from the spinach, then place the leaves in a colander and wash under cold running water. Leave to drain.

2. Melt half of the butter in a large saucepan over a medium heat. Stir in the spinach, with the water still clinging to its leaves, cover and cook for 3—4 minutes, until wilted.

3. Stir in the nutmeg and season to taste with salt and pepper, then reduce the heat to low to keep the spinach warm while you prepare the sauce.

4. Pour the wine and milk into a separate saucepan, bring to the boil, then simmer until reduced slightly. Add the Gorgonzola and stir until melted. Remove from the heat.

5. Beat the egg yolks in a small bowl, stir in a little of the hot sauce, then tip back into the pan with the remaining butter and the spinach. Stir thoroughly and place over a medium heat to warm through.

6. Taste and adjust the seasoning, adding salt and pepper if needed. Serve immediately.

Mama's guide to growing vegetables

They say that man cannot live on bread alone (not even Mama's *superbo* focaccia!) — but it is also true that meat by itself cannot make a meal. Italian cooking is rooted in the land: and that means knowing how to make the best of what nature provides. My *verdura* — my vegetables — are Mama's great secret. From the crunchiest *salade* to the sweetest courgettes, these are what elevate simple suppers to *grande arte*!

And best of all? You can grow them yourself. Nothing — and I mean *niente* — tastes better than home-grown vegetables, picked and prepared and served within minutes... here are Mama's tips for growing three of the best for yourself.

Artichokes

These wonderful plants make beautiful flowers as well as tasting sublime with butter. They can be difficult to grow from seed, so buy as little, poco plants and bed them into a sunny spot in your garden in the spring. If you have access to manure, that will help them grow.

In the first year, it is importante to remove flowerheads — this will help the plant grow strong. After that, the flowers can be lopped off and eaten as they form in the summer. *Delizioso!*

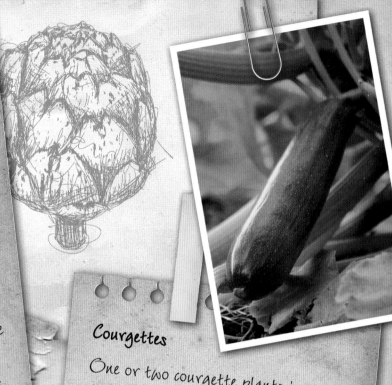

Courgettes

One or two courgette plants in your garden will keep producing all summer long. Plant as seeds into little pots in March and then transplant to a sunny, sheltered spot in May. Allow plenty of room — they can grow *molto grande!*

Keep well watered and pick the courgettes as they appear — the more you harvest, the more they are encouraged to grow! I like them at 10 cm/4 inches long — but you can leave them to become marrows too.

Aubergines

These can be grown on a windowsill if your garden is small or you live in the city — and will provide a taste of Apulia on even the greyest day. Sow a couple of seeds into a little pot in early spring, place a clear plastic bag on top and place on a sunny windowsill until the shoots appear... then remove the bag, and as the plant gets bigger, move to a bigger pot. As they get bigger, support them with a stake, and if you have a garden, move outside in May.

Carciofi alla Romana
Roman-style Artichokes

SERVES 4

1 tbsp lemon juice
4 globe artichokes
6 tbsp finely chopped fresh
flat-leaf parsley
leaves from 8 fresh mint
sprigs, finely chopped
4 large garlic cloves,
2 finely chopped, 2 sliced
200 ml/7 fl oz olive oil
300 ml/10 fl oz dry
white wine
salt and pepper

1. Preheat the oven to 160°C/325°F/Gas Mark 3. Put the lemon juice in a bowl of cold water large enough to hold the artichokes and set aside.

2. To prepare the artichokes, remove all the outer leaves and trim the stalks. Cut off the top of each artichoke and remove and discard the hairy choke. Drop each artichoke in the bowl of lemon water to prevent discoloration.

3. Mix together the parsley, mint, chopped garlic and 3 tablespoons of the oil and season well. Remove the artichokes from the water and drain on kitchen paper.

4. Divide the mint mixture between the artichokes, pressing the filling into each hole left by the chokes. Transfer the artichokes to a deep baking dish that will hold the artichokes upright. Mix together the remaining oil and the wine and pour around the artichokes. Scatter over the sliced garlic and cover with foil. Bake in the preheated oven for 40—50 minutes, until the artichokes are tender. Remove the artichokes from the dish and leave to cool.

5. Transfer the cooking liquid to a small saucepan and boil until reduced by half. Remove the garlic slices, adjust the seasoning and set aside to cool. When both the juices and artichokes are cool, return the artichokes to the sauce, standing upright, and chill for up to 2 days. Remove the artichokes from the refrigerator 15 minutes before serving to bring to room temperature. Serve with the juices spooned over the artichokes.

Scafata
Umbrian-style Broad Beans

SERVES 4

3 tbsp olive oil
1 carrot, finely chopped
1 celery stick, finely chopped
½ onion, finely chopped
4 large tomatoes
350 g/12 oz shelled broad beans,
    thawed if frozen
150 ml/5 fl oz passata
2 tbsp water
4 fresh thyme sprigs
2 bay leaves
pinch of sugar
salt and pepper
extra virgin olive oil,
    to serve (optional)

1. Heat the olive oil in a saucepan over a high heat. Add the carrot, celery and onion and reduce the heat to low. Cover the pan and simmer for 8—10 minutes, or until the onion is soft but not brown.

2. Meanwhile, bring a saucepan of lightly salted water to the boil. Cut an 'X' in the stem end of the tomatoes, add them to the pan of water and blanch for 2—3 minutes, until the skins split. Drain and place under cold running water. Peel and deseed the tomatoes, then chop the flesh.

3. Stir the beans, tomatoes, passata, water, thyme, bay leaves and sugar into the onion mixture. Season with salt and pepper and bring to the boil. Reduce the heat to very low, cover and simmer for 30—40 minutes, until the beans and other vegetables are very tender.

4. Remove the thyme sprigs and bay leaves and adjust the seasoning, if necessary. Spoon into a serving bowl and serve with extra virgin olive oil on the side (if using).

Cicoria con Aglio
Escarole with Garlic

1. Heat the oil in a large frying pan over a medium heat.

2. Add the garlic and stir for 2 minutes, or until fragrant. Take care that the garlic does not burn or over cook.

3. Add the escarole and stir until it is well coated in the oil. Increase the heat to high and continue to stir for 3—5 minutes, or until wilted and tender.

4. Stir in the lemon juice and season with salt and pepper. Serve immediately.

Mama's Tip:
The flavour of escarole can be a little bitter for some tastes so, if you prefer, then you could try using baby spinach instead.

SERVES 4

4 tbsp olive oil
4 garlic cloves, thinly sliced
400 g/14 oz escarole, chicory or radicchio, well rinsed, torn into bite-sized pieces, rinsed and shaken dry
freshly squeezed lemon juice, to taste
salt and pepper

Puré di Patate
Rosemary & Basil Mash

SERVES 4

4 fresh rosemary sprigs
600 g/1 lb 5 oz floury
    potatoes, cut into
    small pieces
small handful of fresh
    basil leaves
125 ml/4 fl oz extra
    virgin olive oil,
    plus extra to taste
salt and pepper

1. Place the rosemary in a large saucepan of lightly salted water and bring to the boil. Bring a smaller saucepan of unsalted water to the boil. Set aside a small bowl of iced water.

2. Add the potatoes to the salted water, bring back to the boil and cook, partially covered, for 20–25 minutes, until very tender but not falling apart. Remove from the heat and leave to cool, without draining.

3. Meanwhile, drop the basil leaves into the unsalted water, push them down with a wooden spoon and boil for just a few seconds until they wilt. Drain and place in the iced water to cool. Remove and pat completely dry with kitchen paper, then finely chop and set aside.

4. Drain the cooled potatoes and rosemary, reserving about 4 tablespoons of the cooking water and the rosemary. Return the potatoes to the pan with the reserved water and season with salt and pepper. Break them up using an electric handheld mixer.

5. When they begin to mash, slowly beat in the oil and then stir in the reserved rosemary and the basil. Adjust the seasoning, if necessary, and serve immediately.

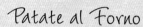

Patate al Forno

Italian-herb Roast Potatoes

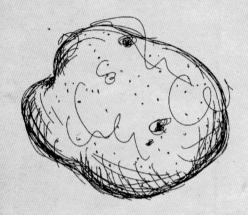

SERVES 4

3 fresh rosemary sprigs, plus
    extra to garnish
800 g/1 lb 12 oz small
    potatoes, cubed
3 garlic cloves, roughly chopped
5 tbsp olive oil, plus extra
    for oiling
salt and pepper

1. Preheat the oven to 200°C/400°F/Gas Mark 6. Brush a large baking dish with oil.

2. Remove the leaves from the rosemary sprigs, discarding the stems, and chop the leaves roughly. Set aside.

3. Place a layer of potatoes in the prepared baking dish, then sprinkle over a little of the garlic and rosemary and season to taste with salt and pepper. Repeat the layers until all the potatoes, garlic and rosemary have been used up.

4. Drizzle over the olive oil, then transfer the dish to the preheated oven and cook, stirring frequently, for 45 minutes, or until the potatoes are tender and lightly browned.

5. Garnish with a rosemary sprig and serve the potatoes immediately, straight from the baking dish.

Mama's Tip:
Substitute some finely chopped fresh mint instead of the rosemary for a fresh-tasting alternative.

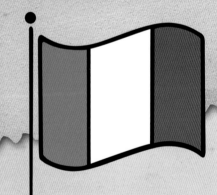

Frittate di Formaggio e Patate
Mini Cheese & Potato Frittatas

1. Bring a saucepan of lightly salted water to the boil. Add the potatoes, bring back to the boil and cook for 12—15 minutes, until tender. Drain well and cool under cold running water.

2. Meanwhile, preheat the oven to 190°C/375°F/Gas Mark 5. Generously grease a 12-hole muffin tin. When the potatoes are cool enough to handle, peel and finely chop them, then squeeze out the excess moisture.

3. Beat together the eggs and milk in a bowl. Stir in the potatoes, red peppers, two thirds of the cheese and all of the chives. Season to taste with salt and pepper.

4. Divide the mixture equally between the holes in the prepared muffin tin, filling each just under half full. Sprinkle the remaining cheese over the tops of the frittatas, taking care not to get it on the edge of the frittatas.

5. Place the tin in the preheated oven and bake for 25—30 minutes, until the frittatas are set and golden brown.

6. Remove the tin from the oven and run a round-bladed knife around each one, then tip them out. Transfer to a platter and either serve immediately or leave to cool to room temperature.

100 g/3½ oz waxy potatoes,
  unpeeled and scrubbed
olive oil or sunflower oil,
  for greasing
4 eggs
125 ml/4 fl oz milk
2 chargrilled red peppers
  in oil, drained and
  finely chopped
85 g/3 oz grated Parmesan cheese
  or pecorino cheese
2 tbsp finely snipped chives
salt and pepper

Mama's Tip:
You can substitute three finely chopped
slices of Parma ham for the red peppers.
Just remember to trim the edge from
each slice before you chop it.

Insalata di Cesare
Caesar Salad

SERVES 4

125 ml/4 fl oz olive oil
2 garlic cloves
5 slices white bread, crusts
  removed, cut into 1-cm/½-inch
  cubes
1 egg
3 Little Gem lettuces
2 tbsp lemon juice
8 canned anchovy fillets,
  drained and roughly chopped
salt and pepper
fresh Parmesan cheese shavings,
  to serve

1. Heat 4 tablespoons of the oil in a heavy-based frying pan. Add the garlic and bread and cook, stirring frequently, for 4—5 minutes until the bread is crisp and golden.

2. Remove the croûtons from the pan with a slotted spoon and drain on kitchen paper. Discard the garlic.

3. Meanwhile, bring a small saucepan of water to the boil. Add the egg and cook for 1 minute, then remove from the pan and set aside.

4. Break apart the lettuces and arrange the leaves in a bowl. In a separate bowl, mix the remaining oil and the lemon juice with salt and pepper to taste.

5. Crack the egg into the lemon dressing and whisk to blend. Pour the dressing over the lettuce and toss well.

6. Add the chopped anchovies and croûtons. Toss the salad again. Sprinkle with Parmesan cheese shavings and serve immediately.

Carpaccio

Carpaccio Salad

1. To make the mayonnaise, finely chop the anchovy fillets on a chopping board, use the tip of a knife to mash them into a paste, then set aside. Put the egg yolk, half of the lemon juice, and pepper to taste into a bowl. Beat with an electric handheld mixer or a hand whisk. Begin to add the olive oil drop by drop, beating constantly, until the mixture thickens.

2. Beat in the reserved oil from the anchovies, then slowly add the remaining olive oil in a slow, steady stream until the mixture thickens. Beat in the anchovies. Taste and add the remaining lemon juice, if desired, and season with salt and pepper. Slowly stir in the boiling water until the mayonnaise is thin enough to just flow off the tip of a spoon. Transfer to a bowl, cover and chill until required. (Leftover mayonnaise can be stored in the refrigerator for up to 3 days.)

SERVES 4

250–350 g/9–12 oz beef fillet,
   sliced wafer thin
2 tbsp tiny capers in brine,
   rinsed and dried
1 tbsp very finely
   chopped shallot
salt and pepper
finely chopped fresh flat-leaf
   parsley, to garnish

ANCHOVY MAYONNAISE
6 anchovy fillets in oil,
   drained, 1 tsp of the oil
   reserved
1 egg yolk, at room
   temperature
1 tsp lemon juice
125 ml/4 fl oz extra virgin
   olive oil
½–2 tbsp boiling water,
   plus extra if needed
salt and pepper

3. Arrange the beef on a serving platter. Sprinkle with the capers and shallot and season with salt and pepper, bearing in mind that the capers are salty.

4. Stir the mayonnaise and thin it with a little extra boiling water if it has thickened. Drizzle over the carpaccio, garnish with parsley and serve.

Mama's Tip:
The best way to get wafer-thin slices of beef is to ask a butcher to do it for you. If you slice it yourself, buy the larger quantity of fillet. Place in the freezer for 20 minutes, then use a very thin, very sharp knife. Layer the pieces of beef between sheets of clingfilm and transfer them directly to the platter, without overlapping.

Insalata di Rucola & Parmigiana

Rocket & Parmesan Salad

SERVES 4

2 handfuls of rocket leaves
1 small fennel bulb
5 tbsp olive oil
2 tbsp balsamic vinegar
50 g/1¼ oz pine nuts
100 g/3½ oz Parmesan cheese shavings
salt and pepper

1. Wash the rocket, discarding any wilted leaves or coarse stems, and pat dry. Divide evenly among four serving plates.

2. Halve the fennel bulb and slice it finely. Arrange the sliced fennel over the rocket.

3. Whisk together the oil and balsamic vinegar with salt and pepper to taste. Drizzle a little of the dressing over each serving.

4. Toast the pine nuts in a dry frying pan over a high heat until golden brown.

5. Top the salad with the Parmesan shavings and the toasted pine nuts. Serve immediately.

Insalata Rustica

Country-style Salad

1. Bring two saucepans of lightly salted water to the boil. Add the potatoes to one pan, bring back to the boil and cook for 20—25 minutes, until tender. Add the cauliflower florets to the other pan, bring back to the boil and cook for 5 minutes, or until tender-crisp.

2. Meanwhile, whisk together the oil, vinegar, and salt and pepper to taste in a serving bowl.

3. Use a large slotted spoon to remove the cauliflower florets from the pan, shaking off the excess water, and stir them into the dressing in the bowl.

4. Drop the beans into the cauliflower cooking water, bring back to the boil and cook for 5 minutes, or until tender-crisp. Drain well, then stir into the serving bowl.

5. Drain the potatoes and cool slightly under cold running water. Peel and cut into bite-sized pieces, then stir into the dressing together with the spring onions and radish. Make sure all the vegetables are coated with dressing, then set aside for at least 1 hour.

6. When ready to serve, line a platter with radicchio leaves. Stir the spinach into the serving bowl and add extra oil, vinegar and salt and pepper, if desired. Stir in the pine nuts and raisins.

7. Spoon the salad onto the radicchio leaves, adding any dressing left in the bowl. Serve with plenty of ciabatta bread to mop up the dressing.

SERVES 4

300 g/10½ oz new potatoes
200 g/7 oz small cauliflower
  florets
4 tbsp extra virgin olive oil,
  plus extra if needed
4½ tsp red wine vinegar,
  plus extra if needed
200 g/7 oz fine French beans,
  cut into bite-sized pieces
4 spring onions, finely chopped
1 radish, thinly sliced
85 g/3 oz baby spinach leaves
2 tbsp toasted pine nuts
2 tbsp raisins or sultanas
salt and pepper
radicchio leaves and ciabatta
  bread, to serve

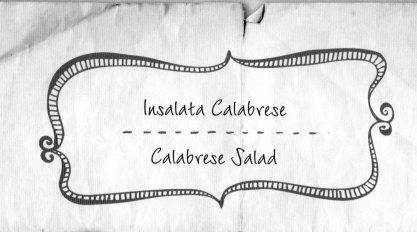

Insalata Calabrese

- - - - - - - - - -

Calabrese Salad

SERVES 4

250 g/9 oz buffalo mozzarella
  cheese, thinly sliced
2 large beef tomatoes, cut into
  5-mm/¼-inch slices
6 large fresh basil leaves
sea salt and pepper
extra virgin olive oil and aged
  balsamic vinegar, to serve

1. Divide the cheese and tomato slices between four plates, arranging them decoratively in a circular wheel shape. Sprinkle with salt and pepper.

2. Lay the basil leaves on top of each other, roll up in a cigar shape and thinly slice crossways to make fine shreds.

3. Sprinkle the basil shreds over the salads and serve immediately, with oil and vinegar drizzled over the top. Place the olive oil and the vinegar on the table so that more can be added, if desired.

Mama's Tip:
In winter when tomatoes are pale and flavourless, this simple salad is better made with sun-dried tomatoes and with snipped chives replacing the basil.

Insalata di Pollo Grigliato e Pesto

Grilled Chicken & Pesto Salad

1. Preheat the grill to medium—high and position the grill rack about 7.5 cm/3 inches below the heat. Brush the chicken thighs with oil and season to taste. Brush the rack with a little oil, add the chicken thighs, skin-side up, and cook for 20—25 minutes, or until the chicken is cooked through and the juices run clear when a skewer is inserted into the thickest part of the meat. Remove from the heat and set aside.

2. Meanwhile, bring a large saucepan of lightly salted water to the boil. Add the pasta, return to the boil and cook for 8—10 minutes, or until tender but still firm to the bite. Add the beans 5 minutes before the end of the cooking time.

3. Drain the pasta and beans, shaking off the excess water, and immediately tip into a large bowl. Add the pesto and stir until the pasta and beans are well coated. Set aside to cool.

4. When the chicken is cool enough to handle, remove the skin and bones and cut the flesh into bite-sized pieces. Stir into the pesto mixture and season to taste with salt and pepper. Set aside to cool completely, then cover and chill until required. (It will keep for up to 1 day, covered, in the refrigerator.)

5. Remove the salad from the refrigerator 10 minutes before serving. Arrange the tomato slices on a serving platter. Stir the salad and add extra pesto, if needed. Mound the salad on top of the tomatoes, garnish with basil leaves and serve immediately.

SERVES 4

4 large chicken thighs
sunflower oil or olive oil,
 for brushing
200 g/7 oz dried trifoli or
 fusilli pasta
200 g/7 oz fine French beans,
 chopped
300 g/10½ oz ready-made pesto,
 plus extra if needed
2 large tomatoes, sliced
salt and pepper
fresh basil leaves, to garnish

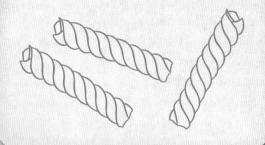

Magnifico Holiday Meals

Holidays! These are the most magical times for a mother (and a grandmother — and especially a great grandmother!). For it is on holidays when all the little chicks come home to Mama's coop. It's a time for the best wines, the tastiest food, for laughter and love. It is a time for families — and for the family cook, it is a time to show the very best of what you can do in the kitchen. If the simplest way I can express my daily love for my family is by putting my heart and soul into every meal I set down before them, then it is on the holidays that I can elevate that love into something *molto speciale*. At Christmas, Easter, New Year's Eve and all the other Carnivales that light up the year like stars across the skies — these are the times when Mama shows just what she has become so loved for, by providing a lovely array of comfort food and sweet treats.

Mama's guide to an Italian Christmas

Buon Natale! Christmas in Italy is a wonderful time — and Christmas in Mama's house in Apulia is the most wonderful place on earth!

Christmas is all about *famiglia* — and Mama is lucky enough to always have the *bambini* around at this time of year — my children, and my children's children, and even their children, my *pronipoti*, will all come together every year to eat, drink, laugh, give thanks and celebrate the season.

In Italy we have many traditions unique to our country: our *bambini*, for instance, don't write letters to Father Christmas asking for the latest electronic gadgets — they write letters to their parents, telling them why they love them.

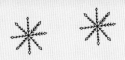

But of course, in Mama's house, when we come together at Christmas, we come together most often around the dinner table. Not just for Christmas dinner (though Mama's Rolled Stuffed Turkey Breast is an unmissable part of the season!) — but for many meals throughout the festive period.

Christmas cooking is not just about *uno grosso meal* — it's about what you cook over the whole season. Clams with Spaghetti or Baked Fish are traditional Christmas Eve dinners. Aubergine Bake is our usual dish to eat on Christmas morning, as we often go to mid-morning Mass and this stops our tummies rumbling during the service!

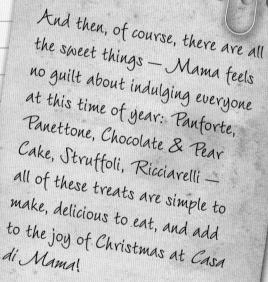

And then, of course, there are all the sweet things — Mama feels no guilt about indulging everyone at this time of year: Panforte, Panettone, Chocolate & Pear Cake, Struffoli, Ricciarelli — all of these treats are simple to make, delicious to eat, and add to the joy of Christmas at Casa di Mama!

1. Preheat the oven to 190°C/375°F/Gas Mark 5. Open out the turkey and cover it with a sheet of clingfilm. Use a meat mallet or rolling pin to pound it into a rectangle no more than 1 cm/½ inch thick. Season with salt and pepper and cover with the ham slices, then set aside.

2. To make the stuffing, heat the oil in a large frying pan over a medium heat. Add the sausage meat and fry, stirring to break it up, for 3—5 minutes, until brown and cooked through. Use a slotted spoon to remove the meat, leaving 1 tablespoon of oil in the pan.

3. Add the shallot to the pan and fry, stirring, for 1—2 minutes, until starting to colour. Stir in the garlic and chilli flakes (if using), and stir for a further 1 minute. Add the breadcrumbs and season to taste with salt and pepper. Stir in the parsley.

4. Place the turkey breast skin-side down on a work surface. Make a cut along the length of the breast, down the centre, without cutting all the way through. Mound the stuffing into the centre, then spread it over the top of the breast leaving a 1-cm/½-inch border all around. Arrange the red pepper slices on top of the stuffing. Roll up the turkey Swiss-roll fashion. Use kitchen string to tie it in three or four places.

5. Add the oil to the pan and heat over a high heat. Add the turkey and fry for 3—5 minutes, or until golden brown. Transfer to a roasting tin and roast in the preheated oven for 35—40 minutes, or until the juices run clear. Transfer to a chopping board, cover with foil and leave to rest for 8—10 minutes before slicing and serving.

SERVES 4-6

1.6 kg/3 lb 8 oz boneless
  turkey breast, butterflied
4-6 slices Parma ham
1 tbsp olive oil
salt and pepper

SAUSAGE & PEPPER STUFFING
1 tbsp olive oil,
  plus extra if needed
200 g/7 oz spicy Italian
  sausage meat, crumbled
1 shallot, finely chopped
2 garlic cloves, chopped
¼ tsp dried chilli flakes
  (optional)
100 g/3½ oz fine breadcrumbs
2 tbsp finely chopped fresh
  flat-leaf parsley
2 chargrilled red peppers
  in olive oil, drained and
  sliced
salt and pepper

Pesce al Forno
Baked Fish

1. Preheat the oven to 220°C/425°F/Gas Mark 7 and grease a roasting dish large enough to hold the fish and potatoes.

2. Arrange the potatoes, garlic and onions in a layer on the bottom of the dish, drizzle over half of the oil and season with salt and pepper. Tightly cover the dish with foil and bake in the preheated oven for 30 minutes, until the potatoes are almost tender.

3. Meanwhile, make three slashes on each side of the fish and rub salt and pepper into the slashes. Divide the thyme sprigs and lemon slices between the fish slashes, then set aside.

4. Reduce the oven temperature to 190°C/375°F/Gas Mark 5. Uncover the dish and stir the olives into the potatoes. Arrange the fish on top, drizzle over the remaining oil, return to the oven and cook for 10 minutes per 2.5 cm/1 inch of fish thickness, or until the fish is cooked through and the flesh flakes easily.

5. Remove the dish from the oven. Fillet and skin the fish and divide the fillets between four warmed plates. Serve with the potatoes, onions and olives, and with lemon wedges for squeezing over.

Mama's Tip:
This dish was invented for Christmas Eve in Italy where people go to Midnight Mass and don't want to eat a heavy meal beforehand. It can be adapted to serve a larger number by scaling up the ingredients and using a second roasting dish.

SERVES 4

500 g/1 lb 2 oz firm, waxy
  potatoes, very thinly sliced
1 large garlic clove, very
  finely chopped
2 onions, thinly sliced
2 tbsp olive oil, plus extra
  for greasing
2 whole sea bass, haddock,
  pollack or red snapper,
  about 400 g/14 oz total
  weight, heads removed,
  scaled, gutted and well
  rinsed
4 fresh thyme sprigs
½ lemon, sliced
150 g/5½ oz black olives,
  stoned and sliced
salt and pepper
lemon wedges, to serve

Spaghetti alle Vongole
Clams with Spaghetti

SERVES 4

1 kg/2 lb 4 oz small live
   clams, scrubbed
350 g/12 oz dried spaghetti
125 ml/4 fl oz olive oil
4 garlic cloves, chopped
125 ml/4 fl oz dry white wine
4 tbsp chopped fresh
   flat-leaf parsley
salt and pepper

1. Discard any clams with broken shells and any that refuse to close when tapped, then set the remainder aside.

2. Bring a large saucepan of heavily salted water to the boil. Add the spaghetti and boil for 2 minutes less than specified in the packet instructions. Set the pasta aside, keeping it in the cooking water.

3. Meanwhile, heat the oil in a large, deep frying pan over a medium heat. Add the garlic and stir for 1 minute, until golden but not brown.

4. Increase the heat to high, add the wine and leave it to bubble for 2 minutes, or until reduced by half. Add the clams and stir for 2—3 minutes, until they open. Discard any clams that remain closed.

5. Add 250 ml/9 fl oz of the pasta cooking water to the clam pan. Use a pasta ladle or tongs to add the pasta to the pan, and cook, stirring, for a further 2 minutes, until the pasta is tender but still firm to the bite.

6. Season to taste with salt and pepper. Stir in the parsley and serve immediately.

bianco

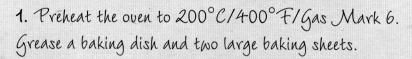

Melanzane alla Parmigiana
Christmas Morning Aubergine Bake

SERVES 6-8

olive oil, for greasing
and brushing
3 aubergines, thinly sliced
300 g/10½ oz mozzarella cheese,
sliced
115 g/4 oz grated Parmesan
cheese
3 tbsp fine dry breadcrumbs
15 g/½ oz butter, melted

TOMATO & BASIL SAUCE

2 tbsp olive oil
4 shallots, finely chopped
2 garlic cloves, finely chopped
400 g/14 oz canned plum tomatoes
1 tsp sugar
8 fresh basil leaves, shredded
salt and pepper

1. Preheat the oven to 200°C/400°F/Gas Mark 6. Grease a baking dish and two large baking sheets.

2. Arrange the aubergine slices in a single layer on the prepared baking sheets. Brush with oil and bake in the preheated oven for 15—20 minutes, until tender. Leave the oven on.

3. Meanwhile, make the sauce. Heat the oil in a saucepan, add the shallots and cook for 5 minutes, until softened. Add the garlic and cook for 1 minute.

4. Add the tomatoes and break them up with a wooden spoon. Stir in the sugar and season to taste with salt and pepper. Bring to the boil, reduce the heat and simmer for about 10 minutes, until thickened. Stir in the basil.

5. Arrange half of the aubergine slices in the base of the prepared dish. Cover with half of the mozzarella, spoon over half of the sauce and sprinkle with half of the Parmesan. Mix the remaining Parmesan with the breadcrumbs. Repeat the layers, ending with the Parmesan mixture. Dot the top with the butter and bake for 25 minutes, until the topping is golden brown. Leave to stand for 5 minutes before serving.

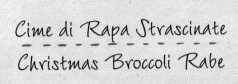

Cime di Rapa Strascinate
Christmas Broccoli Rabe

1. Bring a large saucepan of lightly salted water to the boil. Meanwhile, remove and discard the thick bases of the broccoli rabe stalks and any yellow leaves. Separate the thin stalks with leaves from the thick stalks with flower heads. Rinse well in several changes of cold water.

2. Add the thick stalks to the boiling water and boil for 2 minutes, then add the thin stalks and boil for 6—8 minutes, until all the stalks are tender. Drain well, then set aside.

3. Heat the oil in a large frying pan over a medium—high heat. Add the chopped anchovies, garlic, shallots and chilli flakes and fry, stirring to break down the anchovies, for 2—4 minutes, until the shallots are soft. Make sure that the garlic does not brown.

4. Stir the rabe into the anchovy mixture and season. Stir for 2—3 minutes, until the rabe is reheated and coated in the oil. Transfer the broccoli rabe to a serving platter and spoon over any oil left in the pan. Slice each of the extra anchovy fillets lengthways and arrange on top to garnish.

SERVES 4-6

900 g/2 lb broccoli rabe
2 tbsp olive oil
30 g/1 oz canned anchovy
  fillets in olive oil,
  drained and chopped,
  plus 2 extra fillets to
  garnish
4 large garlic cloves,
  thinly sliced
2 shallots, finely chopped
½ tsp dried red chilli
  flakes, or to taste
salt and pepper

Torta di Cioccolata & Pere
Genoese Chocolate & Pear Cake

1. Preheat the oven to 180°C/350°F/Gas Mark 4. Grease a 20-cm/8-inch loose-based round cake tin and line with baking paper.

2. Melt the butter in a small saucepan, then set aside. Peel and quarter the pears, then remove and discard the cores. Brush the pears with lemon juice and set aside.

3. Put the eggs and sugar into a bowl and beat with an electric handheld mixer for 4—5 minutes, until light and fluffy, but thick enough to leave a trail when the whisk is lifted. Beat in the vanilla extract.

4. Sift in the flour, cocoa powder and baking powder. Lightly and quickly fold in the flour mixture using a large metal spoon. Slowly drizzle the melted butter around the edge of the bowl and gently fold it in, then fold in the hazelnuts.

SERVES 8

75 g/2¾ oz butter, plus extra
  for greasing
2 Conference pears
1 tbsp lemon juice
2 large eggs
115 g/4 oz caster sugar
½ tsp vanilla extract
90 g/3¼ oz Italian 00 flour
  or plain flour
4 tbsp dark cocoa powder
¾ tsp baking powder
75 g/2¾ oz blanched hazelnuts,
  chopped and toasted
icing sugar, to decorate
mascarpone cheese, to serve

5. Pour the mixture into the prepared tin. Arrange the pears, cored side down, in a spoked wheel pattern.

6. Bake in the preheated oven for 35—40 minutes, until firm to the touch and a skewer inserted in the centre comes out clean. Leave to cool in the tin for 5 minutes on a wire rack. Remove the side of the tin and then return the cake to the rack to cool completely.

7. Just before serving, generously dust the top of the cake with icing sugar. Slice and serve with a dollop of mascarpone cheese.

Panettone
Christmas Loaf

SERVES 8

10 cardamom pods
15 g/½ oz butter, plus extra
    for greasing
300 g/10½ oz strong plain
    flour, plus extra for dusting
2 tbsp caster sugar
½ tsp easy-blend dried yeast
1 tsp salt
grated rind of 1 lemon
1 tsp vanilla extract
150 ml/5 fl oz milk
2 egg yolks
55 g/2 oz mixed peel, chopped
115 g/4 oz sultanas

1. Grease an 18-cm/7-inch round cake tin. Crush the cardamom pods lightly in a pestle and mortar and discard the shells. Grind the cardamom seeds to a powder.

2. Rub the butter into the flour in a large bowl and add the sugar, yeast, salt and cardamom powder. Stir to mix. Add the lemon rind, vanilla extract, milk, egg yolks and mix together with a wooden spoon to make a soft dough.

3. Turn the dough out onto a floured work surface and knead for 10 minutes. Return the dough to the bowl, cover with clingfilm and leave to prove in a warm place for 2 hours or until doubled in size.

4. Return the dough to the lightly floured work surface and knock back the dough. Knead in the mixed peel and sultanas until evenly distributed. Transfer to the prepared tin and cover with clingfilm. Leave to prove again for a further 2 hours or until doubled in size.

5. Preheat the oven to 150°C/300°F/Gas Mark 2. Remove the clingfilm from the prepared tin and bake in the preheated oven for 1 hour until dark golden brown. Allow to cool in the tin for 20 minutes before running a palette knife around the tin to loosen. Transfer the cake to a wire rack to cool completely.

Panforte di Siena
— — — — — — — —
Tuscan Christmas Cake

1. Preheat the oven to 180°C/350°F/Gas Mark 4. Line a 20-cm/8-inch loose-based round cake tin with baking paper.

2. Spread out the hazelnuts on a baking sheet and toast in the preheated oven for 10 minutes, until golden brown. Tip them onto a teatowel and rub off the skins.

3. Meanwhile, spread out the almonds on a baking sheet and toast in the oven for 10 minutes, until golden. Watch carefully as they can burn easily.

4. Reduce the oven temperature to 150°C/300°F/Gas Mark 2. Chop all the nuts and place in a large bowl. Add the mixed peel, apricots, pineapple and orange rind to the nuts and mix well.

5. Sift the flour, cocoa, cinnamon, coriander, nutmeg and cloves into the bowl and mix well.

6. Put the caster sugar and honey into a saucepan and set over a low heat, stirring, until the sugar has dissolved. Bring to the boil and cook for 5 minutes, until thickened and beginning to darken. Stir the nut mixture into the saucepan and remove from the heat.

7. Spoon the mixture into the prepared cake tin and smooth the surface. Bake in the oven for 1 hour, then transfer to a wire rack to cool. When cold, carefully remove from the tin and peel off the baking paper.

8. To serve, dust the top of the cake with icing sugar and cut into thin wedges.

SERVES 14

115 g/4 oz hazelnuts
115 g/4 oz almonds
85 g/3 oz mixed peel, chopped
55 g/2 oz ready-to-eat dried
    apricots, finely chopped
55 g/2 oz candied pineapple,
    finely chopped
grated rind of 1 orange
55 g/2 oz plain flour
2 tbsp cocoa powder
1 tsp ground cinnamon
¼ tsp ground coriander
¼ tsp freshly grated nutmeg
¼ tsp ground cloves
115 g/4 oz caster sugar
175 g/6 oz clear honey
icing sugar, for dusting

Mama's Tip:
Panforte is a traditional Christmas dessert from Siena in Tuscany, dating back to the 13th century.

1. Sift together the flour and salt into a large bowl and make a well in the centre. Add the eggs, butter, limoncello and lemon rind to the well, then use your hands to combine all the ingredients to form a soft, sticky dough.

2. Turn out the dough onto a lightly floured surface and knead for about 5 minutes, until firm and smooth. Shape into a ball, wrap in clingfilm and set aside for at least 30 minutes.

3. Divide the dough into eight equal pieces. Work with one piece at a time and keep the remainder covered. On a lightly dusted work surface roll one piece of dough into a thin rope, about 60 cm/24 inches long and slightly more than 5 mm/¼ inch thick. Cut it into 8-mm/⅜-inch pieces then roll each piece into a ball slightly larger than a hazelnut. Set the balls aside and repeat with the remaining dough.

4. Heat enough oil for deep-frying in a heavy-based saucepan over a high heat until it reaches 180–190°C/350–375°F, or until a cube of bread browns in 30 seconds. Add as many dough balls to the pan as will fit without overcrowding and fry for 2½–3½ minutes, until golden but not brown. Use a slotted spoon to transfer the fried balls to a plate lined with kitchen paper. Reheat the oil, if necessary, and repeat until all the dough balls have been fried.

5. Melt the honey in a large saucepan. Add the fried balls and stir. Stir in the peel, half the hundreds and thousands, and the dragées, then place on a plate. Sprinkle over the remaining hundreds and thousands and serve.

SERVES 4

300 g/10½ oz Italian 00 flour
   or plain 0 flour, plus extra
   for dusting
pinch of salt
3 eggs, beaten
40 g/1½ oz butter, diced,
   at room temperature
1½ tbsp limoncello, dry white
   wine or orange juice
finely grated rind of 2 lemons
olive oil or sunflower oil,
   for deep-frying
175 g/6 oz clear honey
4 tbsp finely chopped mixed
   peel
2 tbsp hundreds and thousands
1 tbsp gold or silver dragées

1. Preheat the oven to 150°C/300°F/Gas Mark 2. Line a large baking sheet with baking paper. Put half of the icing sugar into a shallow bowl and set aside.

2. Put the remaining icing sugar, ground almonds, chopped almonds and caster sugar into a large bowl and stir together. Sift in the flour and baking powder and stir to combine.

3. In a separate bowl, beat the egg whites until they hold stiff peaks. Add the almond extract, sprinkle in the cream of tartar and beat again. Beat 2 tablespoons of the egg whites into the almond mixture to loosen, then fold in the remaining egg whites.

4. Use a tablespoon to scoop up a small amount of the mixture, then use another spoon to shape the mixture into an egg shape. Gently drop into

MAKES 22–24

200 g/7 oz icing sugar
200 g/7 oz ground almonds
55 g/2 oz blanched almonds,
  chopped
30 g/1 oz caster sugar
55 g/2 oz Italian 00 flour
  or plain flour
1 tsp baking powder
5 egg whites
¼ tsp almond extract
¼ tsp cream of tartar

the bowl of icing sugar and roll around until it is coated. (Alternatively, shape the mixture into walnut-sized balls and drop them into the icing sugar.)

5. Gently shake the cookie in your hand to reinforce the shape and remove the excess icing sugar. Transfer to the prepared baking sheet and repeat with the remaining mixture until it has all been used. Reserve any leftover icing sugar.

6. Bake in the preheated oven for 15—20 minutes, until set and golden brown. Leave to cool on the baking sheet for 2 minutes, then transfer to a wire rack to cool completely, dusting with any leftover icing sugar. Serve immediately or store in an airtight container for up to 5 days.

Celebrate the holidays — Italian style!

In Italy we take our holidays very seriously. And in Apulia, we are even more serious about making sure our holidays are not only filled with laughter and good times, but also the *cibo migliore*, the very best food!

New Year's Eve

Known as La Festa di San Silvestro, New Year's Eve is a time when the whole family gets together for a huge feast. What do you mean, so soon after Christmas? It's a whole week after! We always eat a meal made with lentils — they symbolise money and good fortune for the coming year. And afterwards — fireworks, music and dancing!

Easter

Next to Christmas, Easter is a time of great celebration in Italy. We have a phrase here, 'Natale con i tuoi, Pasqua con chi vuoi' — Christmas with your family, Easter with your friends. What does that mean for Mama? It means Easter with family and friends! Beautiful Easter Lamb and my famous Florentine Easter Cake are always popular.

Carnevale

How do Italians prepare for Lent? By holding a season of parties and indulgences of course! Carnevale starts on the Feast of the Epiphany, January 6, and lasts until Lent. Across all Italy there are parties, parades and magnificent feasts. In Apulia we are especially famous for our Cenci fritters at this time of year.

Valentine's Day

This beautiful celebration of amore began in Ancient Rome — but in modern Italy the romance of the day is now almost second to a new tradition: that of cooking for each other. We do not do cards or flowers... but something far more special. It is the only day of the year in which Alberto is allowed to prepare dinner for Mama!

Lenticchie San Silvestro

New Year's Eve Lentils

SERVES 4

200 g/7 oz Puy lentils
2 tbsp olive oil
2 celery sticks, chopped
2 leeks, sliced
1 garlic clove, crushed
55 g/2 oz sun-dried tomatoes,
    chopped
2 tbsp chopped fresh sage
1 tbsp chopped fresh rosemary
500 ml/18 fl oz ham or vegetable
    stock
280 g/10 oz bottled artichoke
    hearts, drained
salt and pepper

1. Place the lentils in a saucepan and cover with boiling water. Bring to the boil and boil for 10 minutes. Drain and set aside.

2. Heat the oil in a large frying pan over a medium heat and fry the celery and leeks for 2—3 minutes, until softened but not browned. Stir in the garlic, sun-dried tomatoes, sage and rosemary.

3. Add the cooked lentils, stock and salt and pepper to taste, then bring to the boil. Reduce the heat, cover and simmer gently for 25—30 minutes, or until the lentils are tender.

4. Stir in the artichokes and heat gently for 2—3 minutes. Serve immediately.

Agnello di Pasqua
Easter Roast Lamb

SERVES 6

1.8 kg/4 lb leg of lamb
2 garlic cloves, thinly sliced
2 tbsp rosemary leaves
2 tbsp olive oil
8 tbsp olive oil
900 g/2 lb potatoes,
    cut into 2.5-cm/1-inch cubes
6 fresh sage leaves, chopped
150 ml/5 fl oz Marsala
salt and pepper

1. Preheat the oven to 220°C/425°F/Gas Mark 7. Use a small knife to make incisions all over the lamb, then insert the garlic and about half of the rosemary leaves.

2. Place the lamb in a roasting tin and spoon over half of the oil. Roast in the preheated oven for 15 minutes.

3. Reduce the oven temperature to 180°C/350°F/Gas Mark 4. Remove the lamb from the oven and season to taste with salt and pepper. Turn the lamb over, return to the oven and roast for a further hour.

4. Put the potatoes in a separate roasting tin, add the remaining oil and toss to coat. Sprinkle with the remaining rosemary and the sage. Place the potatoes in the oven with the lamb and roast for 40 minutes.

5. Remove the lamb from the oven, turn it over and pour over the Marsala. Return it to the oven with the potatoes and cook for a further 15 minutes, or until cooked to taste.

6. Transfer the lamb to a carving board and cover with foil. Remove the potatoes and set aside. Place the juices from the meat in a saucepan over a high heat and bring to the boil. Continue to boil until thickened and syrupy. Carve the lamb into slices and serve with the potatoes and meat juices.

Schiacciata
Florentine Easter Cake

1. Grease a 25 x 15-cm/10 x 6-inch baking tin or roasting tin with lard. Stir together the flour, caster sugar, yeast, salt and orange rind in a large bowl. Add the lard and work in until the mixture resembles coarse crumbs. Make a well in the centre, add the orange juice, egg yolks and water and beat together until a soft, sticky dough forms. Slowly add extra water if the dough is too stiff.

2. Turn out the dough onto a floured work surface and knead for 10 minutes until the lard has melted and is distributed and the dough is smooth. Wash and dry the mixing bowl, then grease with lard.

3. Shape the dough into a ball, roll around in the bowl and cover with clingfilm. Set aside in a warm place until doubled in volume, which can take up to 2 hours.

425 g/15 oz Italian 00 flour
  or strong white flour, plus
  extra for dusting
55 g/2 oz caster sugar
7 g/¼ oz easy-blend
  dried yeast
pinch of salt
finely grated rind of
  2 large oranges
55 g/2 oz lard or butter,
  diced, plus extra for
  greasing
3 tbsp freshly squeezed
  orange juice
2 egg yolks, beaten
175-225 ml/6-8 fl oz water,
  heated to 46°C/115°F
icing sugar, to decorate
  (optional)

4. Turn out the dough and lightly knead. Press it into the prepared tin. Cover with a sheet of greased clingfilm and flatten and level the dough to not more than 1 cm/ ½ inch thick. Leave to rise for 20 minutes. Preheat the oven to 190°C/375°F/Gas Mark 5.

5. Remove the clingfilm and bake the cake in the preheated oven for 30—35 minutes, or until it is golden, about 2.5 cm/1 inch high and coming away from the side of the tin. Transfer the tin to a wire rack and thickly dust the top of the cake with icing sugar, if preferred. Leave the cake in the tin on the rack to cool completely.

6. Cut into 12 squares and serve.

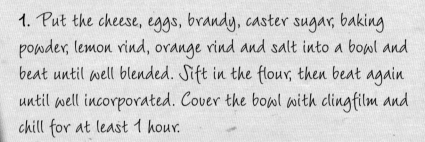

Chiacchiere
Carnival Ricotta Fritters

MAKES 24

300 g/10½ oz ricotta cheese
2 eggs, beaten
3 tbsp brandy or rum
1½ tbsp caster sugar
1½ tbsp baking powder
1 tsp finely grated lemon rind
1 tsp finely grated orange rind
pinch of salt
175 g/6 oz self-raising flour
sunflower oil, for deep-frying,
  plus extra for greasing
icing sugar, to decorate

1. Put the cheese, eggs, brandy, caster sugar, baking powder, lemon rind, orange rind and salt into a bowl and beat until well blended. Sift in the flour, then beat again until well incorporated. Cover the bowl with clingfilm and chill for at least 1 hour.

2. When ready to fry, heat enough oil for deep-frying in a heavy-based saucepan over a high heat until it reaches 180—190°C/350—375°F, or until a cube of bread browns in 30 seconds. Preheat the oven to 150°C/300°F/Gas Mark 2. Line a heatproof plate with kitchen paper and set aside.

3. Grease a large spoon with oil, then use it to drop as many spoonfuls of the mixture into the hot oil that will fit in the pan without overcrowding. Fry for 3—5 minutes, gently turning the fritters over once, until they rise to the surface, puff and turn brown.

4. Use a slotted spoon to remove the fritters from the oil and drain well on kitchen paper. Transfer to the lined plate and keep warm in the oven while you fry the remaining mixture. Reheat the oil between batches and re-grease the spoon, if necessary. When all the mixture has been fried, dust the fritters with icing sugar and serve immediately.

1. Place the sultanas, mixed peel, grappa and lemon rind in a bowl and leave to soak for 1 hour. Place the flour, sugar and yeast in a bowl and stir in the egg with enough of the milk to make a thick batter. Stir the sultana mixture and the pine nuts into the bowl. Cover and leave in a warm place for about 3 hours, or until spongy and doubled in size.

2. When ready to fry, heat enough oil for deep-frying in a heavy-based saucepan over a high heat until it reaches 180–190°C/350–375°F, or until a cube of bread browns in 30 seconds. Preheat the oven to 150°C/300°F/Gas Mark 2. Line a heatproof plate with kitchen paper and set aside.

3. Grease a large spoon with oil, then use it to drop as many spoonfuls of the mixture into the hot oil that will fit in the pan. Fry for 3–5 minutes, turning the fritters over once, until they rise to the surface and turn brown. Use a slotted spoon to remove the fritters and transfer to the lined plate and keep warm in the oven while you fry the remaining mixture. Reheat the oil between batches and re-grease the spoon, if necessary. Dust with icing sugar and serve immediately.

MAKES 24

100 g/3½ oz sultanas
75 g/2¾ oz mixed peel, chopped
3 tbsp grappa or rum
finely grated rind of 1 lemon
400 g/14 oz plain flour
55 g/2 oz caster sugar
7 g/¼ oz easy-blend dried yeast
1 small egg, beaten
about 250 ml/9 fl oz tepid milk
40 g/1½ oz pine nuts
sunflower oil, for deep-frying, plus extra for greasing
icing sugar, for dusting

Delizioso Desserts
& Gelati

Mama once heard a fool declare 'always leave an audience wanting more'. What? These are the words of a miser! Mama never leaves anyone wanting more! It is always a source of constant pride to me that nobody has ever left my table unsatisfied — and, once you learn the secrets of Mama's *delizioso* desserts and gelati, it should be the same for you! Too many cooks think of the dessert as an afterthought to the meal, something that can be squeezed in if there's room. Not so in Italy! Here we think of a dessert as a miniature work of art in itself, as worthy of as much attention and time as anything else you might put on your table. Just think of Biscotti, Zabaglione, Cannoli, Tiramisu . . . or Chocolate Cake, Gelati, Panna Cotta — never let it be said anyone has ever left my table wanting more!

Gelato di Lampone
Raspberry Gelato

1. Check through the raspberries for any imperfections and discard any that are past their best. Hull the remaining raspberries and place in a bowl.

2. Purée the raspberries in a blender or food processor, strain through a fine-meshed, non-metallic sieve to remove all the seeds, then set aside.

3. Put the milk and sugar into a saucepan and place over a medium heat, stirring thoroughly until the sugar dissolves. Put the cornflour into a small bowl and stir in 4 tablespoons of the warm milk, stirring until smooth.

4. Stir the cornflour mixture into the milk pan, increase the heat and stir constantly for 6—8 minutes, until just below boiling point, or until the mixture thickens. If there are any lumps, work through a sieve.

MAKES ABOUT 500 G/1 LB 2 OZ

360 g/12½ oz fresh raspberries
350 ml/12 fl oz milk
55 g/2 oz caster sugar
4½ tsp cornflour

5. Pour the mixture into a bowl, stir in the raspberry purée and leave to cool. Transfer to a freezerproof bowl and freeze. It does not need any beating while it freezes.

6. Transfer to the refrigerator 30 minutes before serving to soften. Serve in small bowls before the gelato gets too soft.

Mama's Tip:
For all my hints and tips on making the perfect gelati then go to pages 194 and 195.

Tartufo

- - - - - - - - - -

Chocolate Ice Cream Balls

1. Place four 150-ml/5-fl oz freezerproof bowls in the freezer.

2. Transfer the ice cream to a large bowl and leave until just beginning to soften, then stir in the chocolate chips. Remove the bowls from the freezer and divide the ice cream mixture between them. Push a cherry into the centre of each and smooth over the hole. Place in the freezer for at least 2 hours, or until firm.

3. Bring a small saucepan of water to simmering point. Working with one bowl at a time, submerge each bowl in the water for 5—10 seconds, until the ice cream looks like it is softening around the edge. Invert the bowl onto a plate, give a good firm shake and the ice cream should drop out. If it doesn't, return the bowl to the water for a further 5 seconds and try again.

4. Sprinkle over a quarter of the chocolate vermicelli and use a small knife to make sure the surface of the ice cream ball is coated. Repeat with the remaining balls.

5. If not serving immediately, place the bowl over the coated ice cream ball and invert the plate. Cover the top with foil and return the ball to the freezer until required.

6. When ready to serve, transfer each ball to a serving bowl and leave to soften for 5—10 minutes. If you want an extra chocolate hit, spoon over some chocolate sauce just before serving.

MAKES 4

600 g/1 lb 5 oz chocolate
  ice cream
100 g/3½ oz plain chocolate
  chips, chopped if large, or
  plain chocolate, chopped
4 glacé cherries
85 g/3 oz chocolate vermicelli
1 quantity Chocolate Sauce,
  see page 198, to serve
  (optional)

Mama's Tip:
Don't allow the ice cream to soften
too much in step 2 before you add
the chocolate chips or they will all
sink to the bottom of the bowl.

Making gorgeous gelati

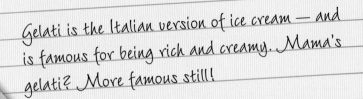

Gelati is the Italian version of ice cream — and is famous for being rich and creamy. Mama's gelati? More famous still!

In the north, gelati is made with an egg custard and includes cream, similar to the ice cream you get in England. In Apulia, however, the gelati does not contain cream or eggs.

The basic ingredients for traditional gelati are whole milk, sugar and cornflour and your choice of flavouring. Because this style of gelati has a lower butterfat content than ice creams made with cream, any flavourings you do add — especially *frutta fresca* or fresh fruit purées — really shine.

Making authentic gelati is quick and easy to do, and even without an ice-cream maker you will get rich and creamy results. And you don't even have to spend time beating the mixture as it freezes!

Two tips from Mama will guarantee success. Do not let the milk boil at any point, as too hot a temperature will destroy the thickening qualities of the cornflour. And always stir a few tablespoonfuls of the hot milk into the cornflour to 'slake' it before adding it to the saucepan. This prevents lumps forming. If lumps do form, however, use a wire whisk to beat the mixture while it heats. If the lumps don't dissolve, strain the mixture through a sieve before you add any flavouring.

Then all you have to do is leave the gelato mixture to cool completely and stir well before putting it in the freezer.

Mama's traditional gelato has a shorter freezer life than custard-based ice creams. The texture is best if it is eaten within three days of freezing. About 20 minutes before you are ready to serve, transfer the gelato to the fridge to soften: in Italy, we like our gelati slightly softer than other ice creams.

Sorbetto di Prosecco alle Uve
Prosecco Sorbet with Grapes

SERVES 4

150 g/5½ oz caster sugar
150 ml/5 fl oz water
thinly pared strip of lemon zest
juice of 1 lemon
350 ml/12 fl oz Prosecco
grapes, halved, and fresh mint
sprigs, to decorate

1. Place the sugar and water in a saucepan with the lemon zest.

2. Stir over a low heat until the sugar dissolves, then boil for 2–3 minutes to reduce by half.

3. Leave to cool and remove the lemon zest.

4. Combine the sugar syrup with the lemon juice and Prosecco, then churn the mixture in an ice-cream maker following the manufacturers' instructions.

5. Alternatively, pour into a freezerproof container and freeze, uncovered, whisking at hourly intervals until frozen.

6. When ready to serve, leave at room temperature to soften slightly, then scoop the sorbet into sundae glasses.

7. Decorate with grape halves and mint sprigs before serving.

Cassata
Sicilian Ice Cream

1. Press the ricotta through a sieve into a bowl using a wooden spoon.

2. Stir in the icing sugar and orange flower water, beating until smooth.

3. Whip the cream until thick enough to hold its shape, then fold into the ricotta mixture.

4. Churn the mixture in an ice-cream maker following the manufacturers' instructions. Alternatively, pour into a freezerproof container and freeze, uncovered, until slushy.

5. Fold in the mixed peel, candied angelica, glacé cherries, chocolate and pistachio nuts.

6. Tip the mixture into a 1.2-litre/2-pint bombe mould or pudding basin and freeze until firm. Leave at room temperature for 10—15 minutes before turning out.

7. Cut the ice cream into wedges and serve on a plate with glacé fruits.

SERVES 6–8

400 g/14 oz ricotta cheese
175 g/6 oz icing sugar
1 tsp orange flower water
200 ml/7 fl oz double cream
100 g/3½ oz mixed peel, chopped
55 g/2 oz candied angelica, chopped
55 g/2 oz glacé cherries, chopped
40 g/1½ oz plain chocolate, chopped
40 g/1½ oz pistachio nuts, chopped
glacé fruits, to serve

Gelato di Pistacchi
Pistachio Gelato

1. Preheat the oven to 180°C/350°F/Gas Mark 4. Bring a saucepan of water to the boil. Add the nuts and boil for 30 seconds. Drain and shake well, then peel off the outer skins. Arrange the nuts on a baking sheet and toast in the preheated oven for 5 minutes. Tip the nuts into a blender or food processor.

2. Pour the milk into a saucepan and heat over a high heat until just below boiling point. Pour about one third of the milk over the nuts and blend the mixture until a thick paste forms. Stir the paste into the pan with the milk, cover and set aside for 4 hours to infuse. Strain, pressing down firmly, then discard the nuts and reserve the liquid.

3. Reheat the pistachio-flavoured liquid over a low heat. Add the sugar and stir until it dissolves. Put the cornflour into a bowl and whisk in 4 tablespoons of the liquid, whisking until smooth. Stir the cornflour mixture into the pan, increase the heat and stir constantly until just below boiling point, then continue to stir for 8—10 minutes, until the mixture thickens. If there are any lumps, work the mixture through a sieve.

4. Pour the mixture into a bowl and leave to cool. Transfer to a freezerproof serving bowl and freeze. Transfer to the refrigerator 30 minutes before serving to soften. Serve scoops in individual bowls.

5. Meanwhile, to make the sauce, gently melt the chocolate in a heatproof bowl set over a saucepan of gently simmering water, stirring until smooth. Stir in the cream, vanilla, butter and salt, stirring until smooth and shiny. Remove from the heat and leave to cool, then spoon over the gelato.

MAKES ABOUT 500 G/1 LB 2 OZ

200 g/7 oz shelled, unsalted
  pistachio nuts
700 ml/1¼ pints milk
85 g/3 oz caster sugar
3 tbsp cornflour

CHOCOLATE SAUCE
175 g/6 oz plain chocolate,
  finely chopped
4 tbsp double cream
¼ tsp vanilla extract
15 g/½ oz unsalted butter
pinch of salt

Mama's Tip:
Peeling the nuts is not totally
necessary, but it does give the
finished dish a clear, fresh
colour. You can skip the step
but the colour will be less
appealing.

Granita di Limone
Lemon Granita

1. Heat the water in a heavy-based saucepan over a low heat. Add the sugar and stir until it has dissolved. Bring to the boil, then remove from the heat and leave to cool.

2. Stir the lemon juice and rind into the cooled syrup.

3. Pour the mixture into a freezerproof container and freeze for 3—4 hours.

4. Remove the container from the freezer and dip the base into hot water. Turn out the ice block and chop roughly, then place in a heavy-duty food processor and process until it forms small crystals.

5. Spoon into sundae glasses and serve immediately.

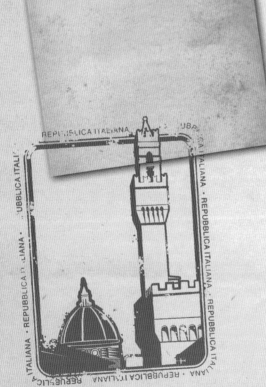

SERVES 4

450 ml/16 fl oz water
115 g/4 oz granulated sugar
225 ml/8 fl oz lemon juice
grated rind of 1 lemon

Cannoli Siciliani
Chocolate Orange Cannoli

1. Beat the egg and Marsala together. Put the flour, sugar and salt into a food processor and blend. With the motor running, slowly pour in the egg mixture until the ingredients just come together to form a dough. Turn out the dough onto a lightly floured work surface and knead. Roll into a ball, wrap in clingfilm and chill for at least 1 hour.

2. Meanwhile, to make the filling, beat together the cheese, brandy and vanilla extract until creamy. Sift in the cocoa powder and icing sugar and stir in the glacé oranges, chocolate, orange rind and cinnamon. Cover and chill until required. Cut the dough into four equal pieces. Use a pasta machine to roll one piece into a strip about 50 cm/20 inches long, or roll out on a lightly floured work surface until the dough is thin enough to see through. Cut out 4-cm/1½-inch squares. Brush some cannoli tubes with oil and diagonally roll a piece of dough around each. Use a dab of water to seal the corners where they meet and press firmly.

3. Heat enough oil for deep-frying until it reaches 180—190°C/ 350—375°F, or until a cube of bread browns in 30 seconds. Add 2 or 3 cannoli tubes at a time and fry until the pastry turns golden brown and crisp. Using a slotted spoon, remove the tubes and drain on kitchen paper. Continue until all the dough is used, gently sliding the shells off the tubes, and re-greasing before using again. Store in an airtight container for up to 3 days until required. Just before serving, use a piping bag or a spoon to fill the tubes from both ends. If you fill the cannoli in advance they will become soggy. Sift over some icing sugar and serve immediately.

MAKES 20-24

1 egg
2 tbsp Marsala
175 g/6 oz Italian 00 flour,
  plus extra for dusting
2 tsp caster sugar
pinch of salt
sunflower oil, for greasing
  and deep-frying
icing sugar, to decorate

CHOCOLATE & ORANGE FILLING
750 g/1 lb 10 oz ricotta
  cheese
2 tbsp brandy
2 tsp vanilla extract
2 tbsp cocoa powder
3 tbsp icing sugar,
  plus extra to decorate
4 tbsp chopped glacé oranges
3 tbsp chopped plain chocolate
finely grated rind of 2 large
  oranges
pinch of ground cinnamon

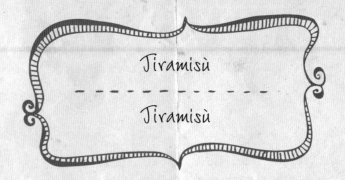

Tiramisù

Tiramisù

1. Whisk the egg yolks with the sugar and vanilla extract in a heatproof bowl set over a saucepan of barely simmering water.

2. When the mixture is pale and the whisk leaves a ribbon trail when lifted, remove the bowl from the heat and set aside to cool. Whisk occasionally to prevent a skin from forming.

3. When the egg yolk mixture is cool, whisk in the mascarpone until thoroughly combined.

4. Whisk the egg whites in a separate, spotlessly clean bowl until they form soft peaks, then gently fold them into the mascarpone mixture.

5. Combine the coffee and rum in a shallow dish. Briefly dip eight of the sponge fingers in the mixture, then arrange in the base of a deep, wide serving dish.

6. Spoon one third of the mascarpone mixture on top, spreading it out evenly. Repeat the layers twice, finishing with the mascarpone mixture. Chill for at least 1 hour.

7. Sift the cocoa evenly over the top and sprinkle with the chocolate. Serve immediately.

SERVES 6

4 egg yolks
100 g/3½ oz caster sugar
1 tsp vanilla extract
500 g/1 lb 2 oz mascarpone
  cheese
2 egg whites
175 ml/6 fl oz strong
  black coffee
125 ml/4 fl oz rum or brandy
24 sponge fingers
2 tbsp cocoa powder
2 tbsp finely grated
  plain chocolate

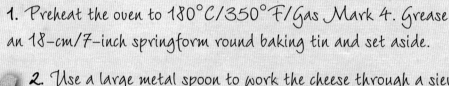

Torta di Ricotta al Forno

Italian-style Cheesecake

SERVES 4-6

butter, for greasing
350 g/12 oz ricotta cheese
3 egg yolks, beaten
100 g/3½ oz caster sugar
4 tbsp Marsala or rum
55 g/2 oz ground almonds
finely grated rind of
    1 lemon or 1 small orange
icing sugar, to decorate

1. Preheat the oven to 180°C/350°F/Gas Mark 4. Grease an 18-cm/7-inch springform round baking tin and set aside.

2. Use a large metal spoon to work the cheese through a sieve into a bowl. Add the egg yolks and caster sugar and beat until blended and the sugar dissolves. Stir in the Marsala, ground almonds and lemon rind.

3. Pour the mixture into the prepared tin and smooth the surface. Bake in the preheated oven for 1—1¼ hours, or until the cheesecake is set and coming away from the side of the tin.

4. Turn off the oven and leave the cheesecake inside for 2—3 hours with the door propped open.

5. When the cheesecake is cool, carefully remove it from the tin and transfer to a serving plate. Dust with icing sugar just before serving.

Panna Cotta con Prugne
Panna Cotta with Spiced Plums

SERVES 4

4 leaves gelatine
300 ml/10 fl oz milk
250 g/9 oz mascarpone cheese
100 g/3½ oz caster sugar
1 vanilla pod, halved lengthways

SPICED PLUMS
8 red plums, halved and stoned
3 tbsp clear honey
1 cinnamon stick
thinly pared strip of orange zest
1 tbsp balsamic vinegar

1. Soak the gelatine leaves in 4 tablespoons of the milk for 10 minutes.

2. Place the remaining milk, the mascarpone, sugar and vanilla pod in a saucepan and heat gently, stirring until smooth, then bring to the boil.

3. Remove from the heat, discard the vanilla pod and add the gelatine mixture, stirring until completely dissolved.

4. Pour into four 200-ml/7-fl oz individual pudding moulds. Leave to chill in the refrigerator until set.

5. To make the spiced plums, place the plums, honey, cinnamon stick, orange zest and vinegar in a saucepan. Cover and cook gently for 10 minutes, or until the plums are tender.

6. Dip the base of each mould quickly in hot water and turn out onto a serving plate.

7. Serve the panna cotta with the spiced plums on the side.

Torta Caprese
Chocolate & Almond Tart

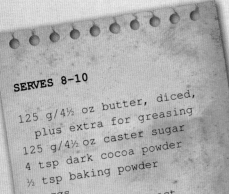

SERVES 8-10

125 g/4½ oz butter, diced,
    plus extra for greasing
125 g/4½ oz caster sugar
4 tsp dark cocoa powder
½ tsp baking powder
4 eggs
¼ tsp vanilla extract
2 tbsp Strega, Marsala or
    orange juice
125 g/4½ oz plain chocolate,
    very finely chopped
200 g/7 oz ground almonds
icing sugar, for dusting
vanilla ice cream or
    mascarpone cheese, to serve

1. Preheat the oven to 180°C/350°F/Gas Mark 4. Grease a 20-cm/8-inch loose-based round cake tin and line with baking paper.

2. Put the butter and sugar into a large bowl and beat with an electric handheld mixer until smooth and creamy. Sift in the cocoa powder and baking powder and beat them in, then add the eggs, one at a time, beating until each is incorporated before adding the next. Beat in the vanilla extract and Strega.

3. Add the chocolate and ground almonds and stir. Pour the mixture into the prepared tin and level the surface.

4. Bake in the preheated oven for 1—1¼ hours, or until firm to the touch and a skewer inserted into the centre comes out clean.

5. Leave to cool for 5 minutes in the tin, then remove from the tin and transfer to a wire rack to cool completely.

6. Just before serving, generously dust the top with icing sugar. Serve with a scoop of vanilla ice cream.

Torta di Cioccolato

Rich Italian Chocolate Cake

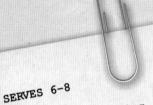

SERVES 6-8

butter, for greasing
flour, for dusting
225 g/8 oz hazelnuts
225 g/8 oz plain chocolate,
  70 per cent cocoa solids
225 g/8 oz blanched almonds
5 tbsp brandy
2 tbsp espresso coffee
1 tsp ground cinnamon
2 tbsp milk
225 g/8 oz caster sugar
5 large eggs, separated,
  at room temperature
mascarpone cheese, to serve

1. Preheat the oven to 180°C/350°F/Gas Mark 4. Grease a 25-cm/10-inch springform round cake tin with butter and sprinkle with flour.

2. Place the hazelnuts on a baking sheet and bake in the preheated oven for 5 minutes, then leave to cool. While the nuts are baking, chop the chocolate into small pieces and place in a food processor with the almonds. Process until the mixture is like breadcrumbs.

3. Transfer the mixture to a bowl and stir in the brandy, coffee, cinnamon, milk and half the of caster sugar. Add the egg yolks, one at a time, and continue to mix. Rub the hazelnuts to remove the skins.

4. Place the hazelnuts in the processor. Process until coarser than the almonds and chocolate. Add to the cake mixture and combine well. In a clean bowl, whisk the egg whites until stiff, add the remaining caster sugar and continue to whisk. Fold the egg whites into the cake mixture with a large metal spoon, a few spoonfuls at a time, with a cutting movement of the spoon so that you don't knock too much air out of the egg whites. Gently spoon the mixture into the prepared cake tin and bake in the centre of the oven for 1 hour, until a skewer inserted into the centre comes out clean. Turn out onto a wire rack to cool. Serve with mascarpone cheese.

Pesche e Amaretti
Peaches with Amaretti

1. Preheat the oven to 180°C/350°F/Gas Mark 4. Lightly grease a baking dish large enough to hold the peach halves in a single layer.

2. Use a small teaspoon to make holes in the centre of each peach half, slightly deeper and wider than the hole made by the stone. Transfer the removed flesh to a bowl.

3. Add the amaretti, egg yolk, butter and half of the sugar to the peach flesh and beat together. Divide this mixture evenly between the peach halves, spooning into a slight mound.

4. Place the filled peach halves in the prepared dish. Pour the wine over and around the halves. Sprinkle the filled peach halves with the remaining sugar.

SERVES 4

4 peaches, halved and stoned
55 g/2 oz amaretti, crushed
1 egg yolk, beaten
30 g/1 oz butter, softened,
  plus extra for greasing
30 g/1 oz soft light
  brown sugar
150 ml/5 fl oz dry white wine
mascarpone cheese, to serve

Bianco

5. Bake in the preheated oven for 25—30 minutes, or until the peaches are tender and starting to brown. Serve immediately, or leave to cool before serving, with mascarpone cheese.

Mama's Tip:
Use Marsala instead of wine if you prefer a sweeter finish - peaches with Marsala is a traditional Italian flavour combination.

Biscotti alle Mandorle
Almond Biscotti

1. Preheat the oven to 180°C/350°F/Gas Mark 4. Line two baking sheets with baking paper.

2. Very roughly chop the almonds, leaving some whole. Mix the flour, sugar, baking powder and cinnamon together in a mixing bowl. Stir in all of the almonds.

3. Beat the eggs with the vanilla extract in a small bowl, then add to the flour mixture and mix together to form a firm dough. Turn the dough out onto a lightly floured surface and knead lightly.

4. Divide the dough in half and shape each piece into a log that is roughly 5 cm/2 inches wide. Transfer to the prepared baking sheets and sprinkle with sugar. Bake in the preheated oven for 20—25 minutes, or until firm.

5. Remove from the oven and leave to cool slightly, then transfer to a chopping board and cut into 1-cm/½-inch slices. Meanwhile, reduce the oven temperature to 160°C/325°F/Gas Mark 3.

6. Arrange the slices, cut-sides down, on the baking sheets. Bake in the preheated oven for 15—20 minutes, until dry and crisp. Transfer to a wire rack to cool.

7. Store in an airtight container for up to 1 week to keep crisp.

MAKES ABOUT 35

250 g/9 oz whole blanched
   almonds
200 g/7 oz plain flour,
   plus extra for dusting
175 g/6 oz caster sugar,
   plus extra for sprinkling
1 tsp baking powder
½ tsp ground cinnamon
2 eggs
2 tsp vanilla extract

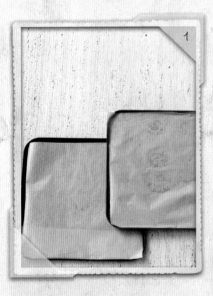

Zabaglione con Frutti d'Estate
Zabaglione with Summer Fruit

1. Put the fruit into a non-metallic bowl and stir in the vanilla sugar and orange rind. Cover with clingfilm and set aside for at least 1 hour.

2. Select a heatproof bowl that will fit in a saucepan over about 5 cm/ 2 inches of boiling water without the base of the bowl touching the water and set aside.

3. Bring a saucepan of water to just below boiling point.

4. Put the egg yolks and sugar into the heatproof bowl and beat with an electric handheld mixer until blended and the sugar has dissolved. Stir in the Marsala.

5. Place the bowl over the simmering water and beat for 5—8 minutes, until the mixture is thick, creamy and holds soft peaks. It is very important that the base of the bowl does not touch the water or the eggs will scramble.

6. Stir the fruit and adjust the vanilla sugar, if necessary. Divide the fruit between four glass bowls and spoon the hot zabaglione over.

7. Serve immediately with ladyfingers on the side.

SERVES 4

250 g/9 oz mixed summer fruit,
  such as hulled, sliced
  strawberries, raspberries,
  blackberries and blueberries
1 tbsp vanilla-flavoured caster
  sugar, or to taste
finely grated rind of 1 orange
3 egg yolks
4 tbsp caster sugar
85 ml/3 fl oz Marsala
ladyfinger biscuits, to serve

Fragole Balsamiche

Strawberries with Balsamic Vinegar

SERVES 4

400 g/14 oz strawberries, plus extra if needed
2 tbsp caster sugar, or to taste
1 tbsp good-quality balsamic vinegar, or to taste
pepper, to serve

1. Pick through the strawberries to ensure all are of the best quality and remove any very soft fruit. Hull and halve the strawberries, placing them in a small bowl as you work.

2. Place the sugar and vinegar into a non-metallic bowl and gently mix together. Add the strawberries and stir to mix together thoroughly. Leave to stand at room temperature for at least 1 hour but not more than 3 hours.

3. When ready to serve, stir again and add extra sugar or vinegar, if desired.

4. Grind some pepper over the top of the strawberries and serve immediately.

220